Pet D

Keeping Ducks As Pets Owner's Manual

Ducks behavior, care, housing, feeding, interacting, breeding, eggs and health all included.

by

Roland Ruthersdale

Published by: IMB Publishing

Table of Contents

Table of Contents

Table of Contents

Foreword

I like my ducks. Actually, I love my ducks! They give me such pleasure each day. I have been a duck keeper for over 25 years and I am sharing my duck knowledge in this book. I hope you like it.

While the love of animals is nearly universal, the different personalities of people affect their approach and attitudes towards pets. Essentially, different people seek different things from pets.

Some people want a furry companion with whom they can cuddle; often, such people find themselves drawn to dogs and cats. Others do not even have the desire to touch their pets and gravitate towards the aquarium hobby.

Some people prefer their pets as domesticated as possible - housetrained, hypoallergenic and tame. Others are fond of animals that not only qualify as wild animals, but also require unusual foods and intensive husbandry to maintain.

Ducks are not capable of becoming house trained, and they often create a bit of a mess, but they are clearly domestic animals, having lived alongside humans for hundreds of years, if not more. However, these robust birds are self-sufficient enough to spread their wings and fly away, if their owner has not clipped their wings.

Once free of the reins of domestication, Ducks carry on virtually as before, though food may be slightly harder to come by.

The most dedicated Duck fans are often keen to learn about, observe and share their cycle of life. Even if no drake is with them, mature female Ducks will deposit eggs. While they will not hatch, they provide educational lessons for youngsters, and delicious eggs for the family.

Ducks can thrive amid relatively simple accommodations, but they are also suitable for free-range keeping in a semi-natural habitat.

Ducks are an important food source around the world. Most of the care information pertaining to Ducks comes from duck farms interested in producing ducks for meat and eggs. It is important to understand that commercial venues do not have the same goals as pet keepers.

While the prime directive of such operations is to maximize profits, the primary goal for pet keepers is to maximize the health and happiness of their companions. Accordingly, some of the recommendations to follow may exceed the minimum necessary requirements to keep a duck alive and fit for consumption. Instead, most of the recommendations to follow will seek to find a balance between the ducks' well-being and the demands on their keepers.

Ducks can make very rewarding pets, but it is important to avoid acquiring one on an impulse. Duck care is not particularly difficult, but it does require significant commitment. Too many people purchase hatchling ducks at fairs or flea markets, only to realize a few weeks later that they are not comfortable providing the care the ducks need.

Contrary to what many in this situation expect, it is not easy to find a new home for your pets. Ultimately, many make the poor (and sometimes illegal) decision to release their ducks to a local pond. This is a terrible practice that must be avoided at all costs.

Ducks are large, imposing waterfowl that colonize new land well. In fragile areas, these domesticated ducks may outcompete or displace native species. This can have ramifications throughout the ecosystem.

Additionally, Ducks that imprinted on humans are unlikely to display the appropriate amount of fear around humans. They may be prone to aggressively begging for food, and ultimately unable to feed themselves adequately. Such ducks are also more likely to be hit by cars, take up residence in inappropriate areas and foul the landscaped and manicured properties in the area.

Accordingly, it is very important to make the decision to add Ducks to your family deliberately, after careful thought and planning. Understand the husbandry requirements of the animals, and the costs you will incur.

When you bring home a duck, it is important to also understand the behavior of the bird. This is especially important if your bird will interact with other pets and animals on your farm. When you have a duck as a pet or even as a business plan, knowing how the duck will react to various situations is an absolute must. If you fail to do so, you will find yourself in many situations that you might not even be prepared for. For instance, if you are not aware of 'imprinting' as a natural phenomenon among ducks, you will be puzzled to find the hatchlings following you all around your home. When you are looking at bringing home any unique bird or animal, just knowing about providing proper care is not good enough. You must also know how to deal with various behavioral changes that may occur over time.

Taking care of the eggs and the hatchlings is just as important as taking care of the adults. If you are not equipped to do this, you will find yourself in a mess of broken and damaged eggs. Of course, the last thing you want is hatchlings that are unable to survive in your care. The care that these delicate creatures require is very different from the adults and you, as the owner must have all the necessary information and knowledge.

Because so many ducks are bought at Easter (and most of these are impulse purchases), many caring and thoughtful breeders refrain from selling hatchlings at this time.

Despite the challenges they present, Ducks make fine pets for those dedicated to their care.

This book covers all the necessary tips and information that you may require if you are bringing home a duck, for either companionship of for your business plans to be successful. This is the complete owner's manual for anyone who finds the Duck to be a fascinating option for a pet.

Chapter 1: Introduction to Ducks as Pets

Having ducks as pets may seem like a rather unusual option to many people. After all, they are not the fuzzy and furry pets that we are used to seeing on a regular basis.

However, when it comes to ducks, there are several other pleasures that owners vouch for when they decide to keep ducks as pets. The most important reason for keeping ducks at home is the fact that they provide the possibility for a lucrative business when they are reared with a purpose.

Having ducks as pets is a pleasure because they are creatures that are very content in a flock. If you are looking at keeping ducks, all you need to do is keep them in pairs or in groups and you will not have to worry about them feeling left out or lonely.

Ducks are extremely non interfering creatures. As long as you have the right environment and the right set up for them, they will not be very hard to take care of. Of course, you are just as responsible towards your ducks as you would be for any other pets. However, with ducks, the advantage is that they are fond of their masters but can also take care of themselves in their master's absence if they have a good flock to tag along with.

When you decide to bring home ducks, there are many things that you have to consider. These pets are not really attention demanding but they require the right kind of environment in order to thrive and be content. A duck is a big investment in terms of the investment. Remember that these creatures are always in the danger of being attacked by predators as they are at the bottom of a food cycle. These birds also carry several parasites that makes them prone to diseases. These diseases are also hazardous for human beings, which means that you need to take a lot more care when you have ducks in your home.

The Purpose of Having Ducks

When you bring home ducks, you must be very clear about the purpose that these ducks will serve in your home. This will help you decide which breed to bring home. There are three main purposes of having ducks at home:

- Duck Farming
- Ornamental Pets
- Creating Hybrids

While duck farming and hybrid creation is very lucrative as a business plan, there are several individuals who simply like to have ducks at home to keep their backyard looking pretty. In the next few sections I will explain each area of interest in greater detail so that you can decide what you want to do with the ducks that you plan to buy.

Duck Farming

The origins of duck farming can be traced back to over thousands of years. Most breeders believe that duck farming started in Southeast Asia. Although ducks have not gained the same popularity as chickens in Western farming, one can see a steady increase in this industry.

Of course, in terms of the type of meat and the convenience of farming, the Western world prefers to rear chickens. However, duck farming is extremely popular in countries like China where they are reared for their eggs, meat and their down. Down, for those of you who are unfamiliar, is soft fur-like layer that you find beneath the feathers of the duck. This is used to make warm clothing in many parts of the world, promoting duck farming in those regions.

It is possible to rear ducks in cages, barn and batteries. Free range is also an option with ducks, especially breeds like the Indian Runner Duck. For those who are looking at making profits by rearing ducks for eggs, this is an elaborate process that requires you to pay close attention to the egg laying patterns of the female ducks. Unlike chickens, ducks are not really reliable when it comes to sitting their eggs and hatching them. In most cases, incubation is mandatory.

Ducks as pets or ornaments

Many people prefer to have ducks as ornaments in their garden or backyard. If you have a large space that is enough for these birds to run and walk around in, you may consider bringing them home as pets. Many people also have their ducks indoors when they have them as pets.

Because of the ornamental value of certain duck breeds, several breeders have worked towards making the breeds of ducks more attractive. Even the color of the plumage has been extensively experimented with to give you the ideal ornamental duck.

It is this quality of the ornamental ducks that also makes it suitable for shows and competitions. If you own ornamental ducks, you can enter your pet in open contests that are not restricted by memberships. Of course, if you are members of associations that specialize in duck breeding, you can enter your beloved pet in more prestigious competitions.
The advantage with a breed that are meant for shows is that they

are not as messy as the other breeds. They are also a lot easier to handle. They love to snuggle up in warm corners of your home, making them perfect indoor pets.

To Create Hybrids

Since ducks are preferred as ornamental pets, several breeders have put in efforts to make the best looking breeds. Even having ducks is a trend that keeps changing globally. The idea is to create novel breeds by mixing great looking breeds and creating ones that have never been seen before.

Duck hybridization is not an easy task considering the sexual behavior of ducks. However, since this is a very lucrative business, it is also an option if you have the resources to experiment with duck breeds.

In the next section, I will take you through the basics of the genetics involved in creating brand new duck breeds. The science might seem extremely simple. However, if you are looking at this business option, you have several professionals who will be willing to provide you with all the assistance you require in the initial years.

Generalized Genetics

Virtually every facet of a duck's growth, appearance and development is controlled by its genetic code. Molecules called deoxyribonucleic acid or DNA for short carry the genetic code. Short, discrete segments of the DNA carry the code for various features of the animal, such as its gender, color and pattern. Many different genes control the colors and patterns of Ducks, and these genes behave in a variety of different ways.

Wild Ducks (and domestic varieties that resemble their wild counterparts) are sometimes called "wild types." These generally have a full complement of "normal" genes, although they exhibit individual variation based on the interaction of the genes.

Through the process of domestication, people changed the appearance of the ducks as they allowed those with positive traits to breed, and culled those which had negative traits. Over countless generations, domestic Ducks diverged slightly from their wild ancestors.

These ducks largely resemble their wild relatives, but they do exhibit a few key differences, such as the loss of white patches on their wings. Additionally, these ducks grow larger than wild Ducks do. Typically, these Ducks are called "black phase."

Later, random mutations appeared in the DNA of some captive Ducks. Some of these traits can be passed on to the duck's offspring, but others are not inheritable and only reflect natural, individual variation.

These heritable genes generally pass from one generation to the next in predictable patterns. Each parent provides half of the DNA necessary to create a new duck, inside each sperm or egg cell. This way, when the sex cell (also called a gamete) reaches its reciprocal cell, the two create a full complement of genetic material, called their genotype.

Accordingly, Ducks usually have two copies of each gene – one from their mother and the other from their father. If these genes are identical – for example, if a duck has two copies of the white gene – the animal is called homozygous. By contrast, animals with two different versions of the same gene are called heterozygous.

A duck's genotype influences its phenotype, by instructing the body on which pigments to make and where to distribute them.

When a duck matures and is ready to breed, it will only include one version of each gene in the sperm or egg cell. Statistically speaking, half of the time the duck will include the genes from its father when making a gamete, while it will provide the mother's version of the gene the other half of the time.

Homozygous animals, which carry two copies of the same gene, have no choice but to display the trait associated with the gene. However, heterozygous animals, that carry two different genes, may or may not display the mutated gene in the phenotype, depending on the type of mutation it is.

Basic Patterns of Inheritance

It is possible to predict the ratio of normal and mutated genes that will usually be present in the offspring of a given pair of adults. To do so, one must know the mutations possessed by the adults, and what the pattern of inheritance associated with those genes is.

It is important to understand that the pattern of inheritance is a statistical phenomenon. Any given clutch may violate the predictions of the model, but given enough eggs, the predictions hold true. Dominant Genes

Dam Sire	Normal	Heterozygous	Homozygous Mutant
Normal	All Normal	50% Normal 50% Heterozygous Mutants	All Heterozygou s Mutants
Heterozygous	50% Normal 50% Heterozygou s Mutants	25% Normal 50% Heterozygous 25% Homozygous	50% Heterozygou s Mutants 50% Homozygous
Homozygous Mutant	All Heterozygou s Mutants	50% Heterozygous Mutant 50% Homozygous Mutant	All Homozygous Mutant

Dominant genes are displayed phenotypically when present. Most of the common traits of a species are dominant, as recessive genes are eventually weeded out of wild gene pools, unless they are neutral (do not cause hardship for those displaying the trait) or offer a selective advantage.

Dominant traits are expressed whether the animal is homozygous or heterozygous. There is no difference in the appearance of the two varieties; the only difference manifests when such animals are bred.

Homozygous mutants only produce other mutants, while heterozygous mutants can produce normal and mutant offspring.

Dominant color patterns of Ducks include the wild-type appearance and the white-headed (Canizie) mutation. Incompletely Dominant Genes

Dam Sire	Normal	Heterozygous	Homozygous Mutant
Normal	All Normal	50% Normal 50% Heterozygous	All Heterozygous
Heterozygous	50% Normal 50% Heterozygous	25% Normal 50% Heterozygous 25%	50% Heterozygous 50% Mutant
Homozygous Mutant	All Heterozygous	50% Heterozygous 50% Homozygous Mutant	All Homozygous Mutant

Incompletely dominant traits express themselves partially when only one copy of the gene is present. When paired with another copy of the gene, such mutations are expressed fully in the animal's phenotype.

Breeding projects involving incomplete dominance can yield animals with three different phenotypes: Normal, heterozygous animals and homozygous mutants.

The blue-dilution and white mutations are both examples of incompletely dominant traits.

Co-Dominant

Dam Sire	Normal	Heterozygous (Intermediate Phenotype)	Homozygous Mutant
Normal	All Normal	50% Normal 50% Heterozygous (Intermediate Phenotype)	All Heterozygous (Intermediate Phenotype)
Heterozygous (Intermediate Phenotype)	50% Normal 50% Heterozygous (Intermediate	25% Normal 50% Heterozygous (Intermediate Phenotype)	50% Heterozygous (Intermediate Phenotype)
Homozygous Mutant	All Heterozygous (Intermediate Phenotype)	50% Normal 50% Heterozygous (Intermediate Phenotype)	All Mutant

Co-dominant traits are very similar to incompletely dominant traits, in that the heterozygous form displays a mutated phenotype.

Co-dominant traits produce animals with intermediate phenotypes. The classic example occurs when red flowers (a co-dominant trait) are crossed with white flowers (another co-dominant trait) to produce pink flowers. Co-dominant traits work somewhat similarly to incompletely dominant traits, as usually the homozygous form of the trait produces an increased effect, relative to heterozygous individuals. These two terms are often confused and misapplied.

There are no truly co-dominant color mutations for Ducks, but the term is sometimes applied to the white and black color forms, because the product of a black and white animal is a "pied" animal that displays both black and white pigment. However, the white color mutation is incompletely dominant, whereas black coloration is dominant.

Simple Recessive

Dam Sire	Normal	Heterozygous	Mutant
Normal	All Normal	50% Normal 50% Heterozygous	All Heterozygo us
Heterozygous	50% Normal 50% Heterozygous	25% Normal 50% Heterozygous 25% Mutant	50% Heterozygo us 50% Mutant
Mutant	All Heterozygous	50% Normal 50% Heterozygous	All Mutant

Recessive traits are only expressed in homozygous individuals, except in the case of sex-linked genes (discussed below).

Heterozygous individuals carry one copy of the mutated gene and may pass it on to their offspring, even though they do not display the gene. In fact, two normal appearing, heterozygous animals can produce young which have both copies of the gene. These homozygous offspring will display the mutated trait, even though their parents looked completely normal.

Simple recessive traits are only visible in homozygous individuals. Unfortunately, there is no way to determine which animals are heterozygous visually. Breeding trials are the only way to be certain that an animal is a heterozygous individual. If an animal produces a mutant, it must be heterozygous for the trait; as such mutations must be passed on by both parents.

In some cases, an animal may be heterozygous for a recessive trait, or it may be completely normal. For example, if a Duclair piebald male mates with a normal-appearing female, all of the young will have one copy of the Duclair gene – making them heterozygous.

If one of these ducklings attains adulthood and breeds a normal partner, some of the resulting offspring will be heterozygous. The problem is, you cannot tell which ones are and which ones are not. Statistically speaking, about half of the offspring are heterozygous, while the other half are not. So, when such young are sold, they are described as being 50 percent possible heterozygous. This means that if you purchase one of these young, there is a 50 percent chance that it carries the Duclair gene.

Similarly, if two heterozygous individuals produce offspring, each individual (other than any homozygous Duclairs) has a 66% chance of being heterozygous.

Simple recessive traits are the most common type of mutation found in Ducks. The barred, brown-rippled, lavender, sepia and Duclair piebald trait are all simple recessive traits.

Sex-Linked Recessive

Dam Sire	Normal (Does Not Display Mutant Trait)	Mutant (Displays Mutant Trait)	Mutation only occurs on the "W" chromosome – there are no homozygous females.
Normal (Does Not Display Mutant Trait)	All Normal	50% Normal Females 50% Heterozygous Males (Do Not Display Mutant Trait)	

Heterozygous (Does Not Display Mutant Trait)	25% Normal Females 25 % Normal Males 25% Mutant Females 25% Heterozygous Males (Do Not Display	25% Normal Females 25% Heterozygous Males (Do Not Display Mutant Trait) 25% Mutant Females 25%	
Mutants	50% Heterozygous Males (Do Not Display Mutant Trait) 50% Mutant Females	All Mutants	

Sex-linked mutations are those that occur on the sex chromosomes. Accordingly, their pattern of inheritance is different for males and females. The chocolate trait is the only sex-linked trait described for Ducks.

Most gene mutations that affect the color of Ducks are located on the autosomal genes. These genes are identical in both males and females, and the pattern of inheritance does not vary between the sexes. In other words, males and females are affected equally by the mutation.

Sex-linked traits work differently. Ducks have genotypically determined gender, meaning that the DNA of the parents determines the sex of the offspring. This contrasts with crocodilians and turtles, whose gender is determined by environmental conditions.

For example, in humans, those with two "X" chromosomes become female, while those that have one "X" chromosome and one "Y" chromosome become male. When adult females produce sex cells, they always receive an "X" chromosome, because that is all the female has to contribute. By contrast, males donate an "X" chromosome about half of the time and a "Y" chromosome the other half of the time. Each sperm cell has one or the other, so male humans determine the gender of their offspring. This is called XY sex determination.

Ducks (and most other birds that have been studied) exhibit a similar system, although key differences exist.

Ducks exhibit ZW sex determination. Females are the heterogametic sex, while males are the homogametic sex. Males have two "W" chromosomes, while females have one "W" chromosome and one "Z" chromosome.

This means that if a mutated gene occurs on the "Z" chromosome, males cannot express the trait. However, it also means that if a trait occurs on the "W" chromosome, females must display it phenotypically, as there is no other gene to express dominance over it.

Males – who possess two "W" chromosomes – may have the mutant trait, but not express it, because it has a normal (and dominant) version of the gene to repress the expression of the mutant.

Ultimately, this means that a female cannot carry a sex-linked trait without expressing it. Males, on the other hand, may very well have the "hidden" trait.

Essentials of Keeping Ducks

Whether you are bringing home a duck for duck farming or to keep it as a pet, there are a few things that are absolutely mandatory:

-        Ducks must have plenty of water around them. Having a duck pond is a great idea as your pets will engage in hunting for frogs and slugs.

-        It is best to bring home pairs or groups of ducks. Ducks prefer to be in the company of other ducks. They feel secure and will remain active when they have the right companions.

-        A coop or shelter is mandatory as ducks are always in danger of falling prey to wild beasts and even your other pets. If you must leave your ducks unsupervised, getting them a coop is a must.

-        Escape is often the leading causes of death in most ducks that are kept as pets. They get out of the enclosure, 'run' away from a source of water, dry out, and die. Either that or running into a busy road. Since these little guys are great escape artists, and don't realize they're likely committing suicide by doing so, a secure, fenced environment is an absolute must.

Chapter 2: Behavior of Ducks

The most difficult thing to understand with ducks is their behavior. Unlike other pets like cats and dogs, these pets are a lot less expressive and are hard to understand. Although ducks have been domesticated for ages, there is no real knowledge about how to understand the behavior of these creatures. In addition to that, ducks are extremely diverse in their behavior. It is impossible to decide which breed to bring home unless you know how each breed behaves. Here are some normal personality traits that you can look for in ducks:

1. General Personality of Ducks

Of all the breeds of ducks that are seen on farms and in gardens, certain breeds like the Indian Runner Duck are extremely very entertaining. If you are simple looking for a companion, you must look for a breed that is highly active, foraging and running around in your garden.

As for the general personality of ducks, several owners might refer to these ducks are 'jerks'. Of course, they are not your quintessential lap pet. However, ducks are very moody and can make excellent companions. If you spend time with them and allow them into the indoors, they will snuggle and cuddle with you. But remember, they must initiate snuggling, not you.

Most ducks are usually quite calm and are very easy to handle. Like most other pets, it is possible to train the certain breeds of ducks as well. If you are looking for a duck that is personable in a way, you can even teach most domestic ducks if you start early enough. It is quite easy if you have the patience to actually spend time training your duck. Of course, you must also give your duck enough space to feel comfortable.

Most domestic ducks are usually calm and will mind their business unless you excite them for no reason. For instance, if your ducks have settled down and you suddenly switch a light on, expect them to be vocal and loud about it. They don't even like to be cornered and will panic when they are. Quite frankly, who likes to be cornered, anyway?

2. Vocalization

Ducks are highly communicative creatures. Certain breeds like the Mallard Ducks and the Indian Runner Duck, in particular loves to communicate and is quite vocal. With familiarity, these ducks will also respond to calls of their owners.

You will notice that it is usually the female that resorts to loud quacks. The male usually only creates a sound that seems like a hoarse whisper. These ducks are much less noisy than a call duck. However, they can make quite a rattle when they are excited, playful or even agitated.

Ducks can resort to a wide range of calls including coos, grunts and whistles. In some rare cases they will also yodel. All in all, you can be sure that your pet duck will talk to you and communicate with you on a regular basis. So, they do make great pets and provide a very comforting companionship.

3. Sociability

Domestic Ducks are quite social. They are friendly and can be tamed to be timid. However, the nature of your duck depends on several things. Usually the biggest difference comes with the gender of the birds. Males tend to be more dominating and are extremely territorial. The females, on the other hand, are quite pleasant in their nature.

Indian Runner Ducks are known to get severely attached to one person. Sometimes, they may even take a liking to your other pets. They will follow the person or pet that they are attached to. They will also be extremely possessive. If the person whom these ducks get attached to, fondle or fuss over someone else before them, they will show you who the real boss is! Sometimes, they will also get violent. They are known to chase and bite when they are hungry or even agitated.

All in all, Indian Ducks are extremely sociable and will only react unusually to sudden and unwanted changes in their immediate environment. Indian Runner Ducks are best when they are in groups. It is never advisable to keep single ducks at home. You can have a few males and females in the group in order to create familiarity and to also promote breeding.

4. Habitat of Ducks

Ducks are believed to be the most adaptable of all the domestic poultry species. These birds not only inhabit several countries in the Northern and Southern Hemispheres, but also inhabit several climatically diverse regions. Whether it is the cold Arctic Tundra or the subtropical parts of the world, Ducks are able to live in various habitats.

They are found both in salt water and the fresh water wetlands. Usually, Ducks prefer to live in the Wetlands in order to feed and forage. They are also found in parks, lakes, estuaries, rivers and small water inlets. Sometimes Ducks are also found in the open sea, close to the coastline. Usually, Buff Orpington Ducks choose waters with a depth of less than 1 metre. They avoid areas that are too deep. If there is aquatic vegetation near a water body, it is likely that you will find a larger population of Buff Orpington Ducks there.

The reason most ducks are found in a wetland habitat is that wetlands are easily the most productive of all the ecosystems. In this habitat you will find several organisms that are living in perfect harmony and are also benefiting from one another. The wetlands are a very important part of nature as they improve the quality of life on earth.

If you plan to rear ducks in your home, you must make sure that you at least provide them with an artificial pond or water body where they can forage and live comfortably. Good water for swimming is a survival requirement for a duck. We will discuss the options for creating the perfect environment for your duck in the following chapters.

5. Compatibility of Ducks

When you bring home ducks, you must also consider their ability to mingle with your neighbors and other pets that you have at home. There are some breeds that are extremely compatible while there are others that are a little more difficult to keep in your back yard. I will give you a list of ducks that you can keep in your backyard and others that are only meant for business. Here are some compatibility considerations that you must take into account before you bring ducks home.

Ducks and other poultry

In most farms, ducks and chickens are bred together. Separation is a good idea, although there are several breeders who will suggest otherwise. When ducks and hens are kept in the same enclosure, there will definitely be squabbles, as there are squabbles amongst their own kind. While most of us might assume that the larger birds, the runners, might harm the chickens, it is quite contrary. Chickens are the ones with sharper beaks and are more prone to attacking and causing damage to your ducks.

If you insist on keeping them in the same enclosure, make sure that they are in a large space. So, if they ever get into a fight, they will have space to move away from each other. Usually, with ample supply of food and water, the hens and ducks will mind their own business and will seldom get in each other's way.

Now, housing is a primary concern with ducks and hens. Only if they have separate housing spaces should you keep the ducks and hens together. Unlike hens, ducks do not always settle down after sunset. They will take some time to roost. Also, during the breeding season, cockerels and drakes might become argumentative if they do not have enough space for themselves.

The feeders for the ducks and hens must be separated. This is because the food that you give your hens is quite different from the food that the Indian runners require. Waterers must, most definitely, be separate. Hens only drink from the waterers and get on with their business. On the other hand, ducks need to take a dip occasionally and will make a mess of the waterer if it is common. So, the water source for the ducks and hens must be placed at a considerable distance from each other.

If you see signs of violence that leads to wounds, you might want to separate their enclosure. You can even restrict the entry from one area to another using wiring and fences. Whether you want to permanently separate the two or only keep them away for particular seasons, you have necessary fencing options.

Ducks and Neighbors

If you plan to have Ducks in your backyard, you might want to be a little more responsible about it. Ducks can be quite noisy, especially females. Like we mentioned in the earlier chapters, it is only the females that make loud quacking noises.

There are ways you can prevent too much noise for your neighbors. First, having thick landscaping around your garden will act as a great insulation against the sound. Second, having Indian Runners in groups will reduce the noise to a large extent. Usually, females become noisy only when they are calling out their mates.

It is a good idea to check with your local Environmental Health Department to check if your backyard is a suitable place for the ducks. If it is an inhospitable environment, expect your ducks to become noisy. You might also want to send your neighbors a circular informing them about the ducks that you might have in your yard. This will also prepare them for an odd quack here and there.

When you have taken care of all these factors, you can be sure that the ducks you bring home will be physically and mentally fit. They will also remain active and will keep you entertained, too.

Ducks and Other Pets

Most Domestic Ducks are rather pleasant creatures to have around. If you have other pets at home, you must make sure that in the first few months of the ducks' arrival, the interactions between your pets and the new entrants is always supervised.

You must make observations of the behavior of the ducks around your pets and vice versa. If you feel like there is any obvious tension or dislike between the animals, do not force them to be in the same space. This can be dangerous to both creatures. Remember, some ducks can be are also highly territorial and can get violent when they are threatened.

Ducks when kept in pairs or groups will seldom bother the other pets in your home. However, there are several instances of great friendships between runners and other pets. If they have grown up together, especially, they will be able to bond with each other.

Chapter 3: Top 5 Duck Breeds to Bring Home

There are certain breeds of ducks that are most preferred across the globe for some obvious reasons. Here are five breeds that you may consider bringing home if you are planning to own ducks for the first time ever.

1. Indian Runner Ducks

Appearance:

These ducks come in a variety of colors like white, fawn, black and trout. The best thing about these ducks is their upright posture. They look really entertaining with their vertical gait. They have long bodies and resemble penguins. This is one reason why they are known as "penguin ducks"

This is a duck that is upright in its posture, almost like the penguin. In addition to that, these ducks don't waddle, they run! Of course, that is how they get their name. Sometimes, they are also called 'penguin ducks' because of their posture.

For those who are keen on having ducks in their farm or garden, the Indian Runner Duck would be the perfect choice, given the shape and the nature of these birds. Not only are they great entertainers, they are also great for a lucrative business.

The elegant and slim Indian Runner Duck is an extremely unique breed of duck and although there is huge debate regarding their origin, (with many enthusiasts believing they were bred for their beauty and uniqueness rather than evolving from natural selection over a period of time) one thing is for sure – top breeders and associations around the world agree that it is vital the purity of the Indian runner duck breed is protected not only for their highly prized personalities and staggering movements – but for their amazing laying abilities that you can convert

into a profitable business.

In many ways, the Indian Runner Duck is the perfect farm or backyard duck that you can have.

Pros:

- Prolific egg layers
- Less Noisy
- Highly personable

Cons:

- Foraging which ruins your backyard
- Maintenance

2. Mallard Ducks

Description

A Mallard Duck is a medium sized bird that is considered to be slightly larger than regular dabbling ducks. Usually, a Mallard Duck will reach an average length of about 50 to 65 cms. The wingspan of a Mallard Duck is about 81 to 98 cms. The Mallard Duck, which is counted among the heaviest of all the dabbling ducks is usually about 0.72 to 1.6 kilos or about 1/6 to 3.5 lbs in weight.

Male mallards will have a very glossy bottle greed head and will have a distinct white collar that distinguishes his body from his head. The chest has a beautiful purple tinge. The wings are usually grey brown while the belly is pale grey in color. The dark tail is characteristic of a Mallard Duck. His rear is usually black in color.

A mottled plumage is very typical in a female Mallard duck. The feathers show an obvious contrast between each other. Like all other dabbling ducks, female Mallard Ducks are also brown or buff in color. The eyebrows, throat and the neck are buff in color while the eye stripe and the crown are darker in color.

34

The one similarity between the males and the females is that they have a speculum patch. In the inner remiges, you will notice a patch of blue feathers that are purple blue in color. These iridescent feathers make the Mallard Duck extremely attractive to look at. These feathers become very prominent when the birds are in flight. Only during the summer molting, these plumes are shed completely.

Pros:

- Prolific egg layers
- Very ornamental

Cons:

- Very anxious
- Noisy breed

3. Pekin Ducks

Description

The Pekin Duck is a pure white duck that is one of the most popular breeds in the commercial market in the United States. This duck breed has been highly domesticated and is a favorite amongst people who are interested in having ducks to build a lucrative business. The Pekin Duck is also considered to have the most delicious flesh in comparison to all its contemporaries. The advantage of having this breed in your backyard is that it is not only very hardy but it also grows really fast, in size as well as in numbers.

The Pekin Duck is creamy white in color. The whiteness of the feathers when combined with the fluffiness makes this bird one of the cuddliest pets that you could ever bring home. Sometimes, the plumage may have a yellowish tinge.

Pekin Ducks serve a dual purpose when it comes to the commercial aspect. These birds are also prolific egg layers which means that those who are not keen on using the meat of these beautiful white ducks can have a lucrative business by rearing Pekin Ducks in their backyard. These ducks can easily lay close to 150 eggs in one breeding season, making it very easy for you to take care of at least all the expenses involved in maintaining these ducks.

The Pekin Ducks is also a great breed for those who are interested in having pets. They are beautiful birds who make great ornaments in gardens and backyards. Additionally, they have a very calm and gentle nature that will make you fall in love with these birds from the moment you bring them to your home.

Pros:

- Prolific egg layers
- Very ornamental
- Less Noisy
- Great Meat Quality

Cons:

- Easily scared
- Prone to Diseases

4. Campbell Ducks

Appearance

Campbell Ducks make great pets as they are gentle and very loving creatures. However, the main purpose of owning Campbell Ducks for most breeders is the lucrative egg business that one can have thanks to the prolific laying abilities of the duck.

The first thing that you will notice about a healthy Campbell Duck is its gait. These ducks are not horizontal to the ground when they are out of the water. These ducks have an almost upright position that makes them appear very penguin like. This is a quality that these ducks have inherited from their Indian Runner Duck ancestors.

The Campbell Duck is not a very heavy bird. Although they are large in size, these birds are usually light weight. A fully grown Campbell Duck usually weighs between 3 to 5 pounds or about 2 to 4 kilos. These ducks are ideal for your backyard as they are the perfect size required. They are also great for commercial purposes because of their size which makes them very easy to handle.

These ducks are descendants of the beautifully colored Mallard Ducks and the Rouen Ducks. Needless to say, the Campbell Duck is also beautifully colored. The Campbell Duck usually comes in four colors: pied, white, dark and khaki. The first ever created Campbell Duck was Khaki in color and hence, this is the most widely preferred color of this duck.

Campbell Ducks are highly active birds. They love to run around and forage through your yard. They are also very agile swimmers. These physical activities of the bird are accompanied by a body structure that supports them. Typically, the body of the Campbell Duck is extremely slender. This means that the duck's body is streamlined. The head of the duck is long and slender and the neck is also very lean. The carriage of the body, as I mentioned before is similar to the Indian Runners. Although it is not perfectly upright, the body is easily about 20 to 40 degrees higher than the horizontal plane.

Pros:

- Most Prolific egg layers
- Less Noisy
- Great Meat Quality
- Calm and Peaceful

Cons:

- Ordinary in appearance

5. Muscovy Ducks

Appearance

Muscovy ducks are large, semi-aquatic waterfowl. The males may reach 31-inches (80 centimeters) in length, while the females top out at about 23.5-inches (60 centimeters) in length. The females usually weigh about 4 or 5 pounds (approximately 2 kilograms), although large individuals may reach 8 pounds (3.6 kilograms). Males are nearly twice as large, weighing up to 15 pounds (approximately 7 kilograms). Large male Muscovies may have wingspans that slightly exceed 5-feet in length (152 centimeters).

Wild Muscovy ducks have pink-colored bills with plentiful dark markings. The tip of the beak features a pointed projection that aids their foraging and preening activities, called the bean or nail.

The Muscovy ducks' most obvious external feature is found on the sides of the face and near the base of the bill called caruncles, Muscovies have numerous warty tubercles on their face, which somewhat resemble the wattle of roosters. The amount of caruncled skin varies between individuals and the genders. Males often feature extensive areas of caruncled skin, while females often have fewer caruncles, and some are almost entirely without the protrusions. Males have a large, fleshy knob at the base of their bill, which females generally lack.

The caruncled skin varies in color as well. This skin is usually black in Wild Muscovies, but in domestic varieties this skin is usually red.

Wild Muscovies have brown-colored eyes, but the eyes of domestic varieties vary in color. Many light-colored Muscovies have blue eyes.

Males have a crest of long feathers that adorns the top of their heads. Usually, the crest lies flat against the skull and is rather inconspicuous, but the males will raise their crests during breeding and territorial displays. Females lack this crest entirely.

Pros
- Good Egg Layers
- Known for their meat

Cons
- Too Large
- Considered too ordinary for ornamental purposes

These ducks are popular as they provide the perfect combination of a domestic duck and also a commercial duck. However, there are several breeds that you can look for on the internet. When you choose, make sure you look for a duck that suits all your needs.

Chapter 4: Bringing a duck home

Now that you know the basics of Ducks, and have been tempted by the myriad of colors and patterns that the ducks come in, you must decide if they are a good fit for you and your family.

1. Understanding the Commitment

Ducks can make wonderful companions, but they are not good pets for everyone. Keeping any animal is a serious commitment, and Ducks are no exception. Be sure that you understand exactly what your responsibilities will be and that you are willing to perform them before adding a duck to your family.

You will have to purchase commercial food for your Ducks, and give it to them daily. Additionally, you will need to provide your ducks with regular access to a place to forage for grasses, seeds and invertebrates. You may also have to confine the ducks to a pen or roost each night and then release them in the morning. It can take quite some time to coral the ducks, although some learn to anticipate the daily activity and may do so with little encouragement from you.

Your ducks will need a safe and appropriate place to live. While some people may have ample space and the appropriate type of setting to allow their ducks to range freely, others may have to construct a pen to contain them. They will also need windbreaks and shelters to keep them from being exposed to rain or cold winds. Finally, while Ducks are not as aquatic as Duck-derived breeds are, they still desire at a small pond for swimming and bathing.

You will have to keep your Ducks' living area and pond clean, which can take a significant amount of effort. Ducks, like all ducks, eat a lot of food and produce an equally impressive amount of waste. While this waste is biodegradable, the process of biodegradation takes some time to occur.

If you only have a few ducks and they live in a very large area, their waste may breakdown fast enough to avoid accumulating. However, in most scenarios, you will be forced to remove this waste on a regular basis. While duck droppings are a nutritious additive for lawns and compost heaps, the sheer volume of droppings produced by the ducks may challenge your patience and commitment.

You will have to find a veterinarian that is qualified to care for your ducks, should any of them become sick. You will also have to do something with the endless eggs that the ducks deposit; and, if a drake is kept with the ducks, the large number of ducklings that will emerge from those eggs.

If one of the ducks gets sick, you will have to arrange for prompt treatment and, often, a separate living area. This will help keep the ducks from spreading diseases among themselves.

2. Geographic Concerns

Temperature

Because wild Ducks are native to the tropics, they are usually quite comfortable living in warm climates. However, it is always imperative to provide the birds with deep shade and a swimming pool during hot weather.

Ducks are also quite cold hardy, and more resistant to cold temperatures than chickens are. However, they do require warm sleeping quarters during the winter if the external temperatures fall too low. Nevertheless, research has demonstrated that Ducks vary the metabolic processes of their muscles and livers to offset and acclimate to cold temperatures (Fernando GogliAntonia Lanni, 1993).

If you live at northern latitudes, you may have to create structures in which the ducks can retreat from the cold. In extremely cold climates, it may be necessary to place heat lamps in the shelter. Another problem faces keepers of Ducks that live in cold climates; you must find some way of converting their water reservoir from an ice skating rink, back into a pond each morning. While water reservoirs in moderate climates may only freeze at the surface, and can be easily broken or melted to provide water access for the ducks, ponds in very cold regions are likely to freeze solidly. It requires a great deal of energy to melt such ponds, so be sure you have devised a plan to deal with this situation before you add Ducks to your family.

Rainfall and Humidity

Ducks hail from relatively humid environments with ample rainfall, so they are likely to thrive in even the rainiest climates.

In contrast, they are not specifically adapted to arid habitats, but given a large water reservoir, they are unlikely to suffer from any humidity-related problems.

Social and Legal Considerations

Ducks are so hardy, adaptable and loved by humans that they have colonized a number of areas outside their natural range. In the United States, both Florida and Texas have breeding populations of the birds. Similar feral populations have been reported in Canada and Europe as well.

Many wildlife professionals consider Ducks to be a potentially problematic addition to natural ecosystems. While no evidence of Duck-caused harm has been collected yet, these large, robust and prolific waterfowl may indeed outcompete many native species.

This has led some jurisdictions to place restrictions on the keeping of Ducks. Always check with your local animal control office, wildlife management department or law enforcement agency before acquiring Ducks. Even if Ducks are legal in your area, it is important that Ducks are not allowed to escape, nor should they be purposely released, to avoid exacerbating this problem.

Even if Ducks are not able to colonize your area, they may spread disease to other species of waterfowl, before they pass away or move. This can cause potentially catastrophic results for wild ecosystems.

3. Pros and Cons

Pros	Cons
Ducks are highly decorative because of their colorful plumage.	Duck females and juvenile males are capable of flight, unless their wings are clipped or pinioned.
Ducks live for about 8 years.	Ducks are much larger than the more commonly kept, white Ducks.
In contrast to Ducks and other breeds derived from wild Ducks, Ducks do not spend as much time in the water.	Handling Ducks is difficult, potentially dangerous and stressful for the birds. They are very noisy and loud. Care must be exercised when restraining or manipulating adult birds.
Migration is not a regular part of the Duck lifecycle, although they will move short distances to avoid inclement weather.	Ducks are prone to pecking their cagemates when overcrowded.
Many people find that their Ducks become very tame, friendly companions.	Ducks may sometimes be aggressive.

Ducks are prolific egg layers that will keep your family stocked in eggs.	Ducks are prolific egg layers that may produce more eggs or chicks than you can easily accommodate.

4. Myths and Misinformation

Myth: *Ducks are mean and aggressive.*

Fact: Male Ducks are aggressive towards each other, and some drakes do react aggressively towards humans. However, most drakes become friendly, loyal companions if raised with love and attention from a young age. Most female Ducks are very gentle with people.

Part of their aggressive reputation may stem from their large size, which can be intimidating to some. Combined with the aggressive begging habits of feral ducks and their unusual appearance, it is easy to understand how this largely misguided reputation came to be.

Myth: *You can get rich breeding Ducks.*

Fact: While you can certainly raise and breed Ducks with relative ease, you are highly unlikely to generate a significant revenue stream from a flock of pet ducks. Even if you have three female ducks, and each lays 100 eggs in a year, you only have 300 eggs. Most large-scale commercial productions produce millions of ducks annually. To say you are at a competitive disadvantage would be an understatement.

Myth: *Ducks can live inside as dogs or cats can.*

Fact: The Center for Disease Control and Prevention strongly cautions against keeping poultry in living spaces. Among other problems, ducks can transmit Salmonella to their human keepers. Salmonella may only cause healthy adults some gastrointestinal distress, but it can be fatal for children and the elderly. Your ducks can be part of the family, but they belong outside (or in dedicated buildings).

Myth: *If you touch a ducks caruncled skin, you will get warts.*

Fact: Utterly false. The caruncled skin is completely harmless to touch. It feels soft, dry and somewhat rubbery. However, as with any other animal, you should always wash your hands with soap and water after touching Ducks.

Myth: *Ducks will always stay in your yard if you feed them well.*

Fact: While it is true that Ducks tend to stay in the same area as long as their needs are met, and they do not migrate, nothing prevents them from flying away. Clipping or pinioning their wings does prevent them from flying, but is an undesirable option in the minds of some. Each keeper will have to decide if their ducks' wings will be altered or if they can live with the relatively remote possibility that the birds will fly off.

Myth: *When you breed two Ducks of different colors, their offspring will exhibit a blend of their colors.*

Fact: In some cases, such as the offspring from one black parent and one white parent, the offspring will exhibit varying amounts of black and white pigment. However, the various color mutations of the species work in a variety of ways. By understanding the pattern of inheritance among the various colors, it is possible to predict the type of offspring a given pair will produce.

Myth: *If your ducks look healthy and clean, they are probably free from diseases.*

Fact: Nothing could be further from the truth. Often, ducks carry sub-clinical infestations of bacteria, viruses or protozoa. While they may not be suffering from the symptoms that are characteristic of the disease, they may still harbor the pathogen and be able to spread it.

Salmonella is an excellent example of such a disease. Most ducks probably harbor the bacteria in their bodies, yet they often exhibit no outward signs of illness. Nevertheless, these animals can spread the infection to humans and other animals. Accordingly, strict hygiene is always required when caring for ducks.

5. Seasonal Care for Ducks

The requirements of your pet duck change according to the season. You must be prepared to make necessary changes in the feeding, bedding and even shelter of your ducks to make sure that they are able to get through a particular season comfortably.

Of course ducks come with natural thermoregulation, thanks to the waterproofing of their plumage. However there are several other things that the owner must take care of to ensure that the ducks are healthy

Summer Care for Ducks

During the summer months, you must be aware that the ducks will start laying eggs. So the first thing that you must take care of is the bedding of the duck or the nest. If you are able to provide a nest or bedding that is additionally cushiony, you can prevent damage to the eggs. In addition to that, you must also increase the litter on the floor of the coop.

The food that you give your duck will change in the summer months. For the ducks that are about to lay eggs, you must make sure you mix in layers pellets instead of regular duck feed pellets.

The shelter does not require any additional insulation in the summer months. However, you must be very careful with the sun exposure of your ducks. Make sure that they have ample shade from the blistering heat of the sun. There have been several instances when ducks have had sunstrokes because they did not get enough sunlight. You must also keep plenty of clean water around so that the ducks can cool themselves off when required.

Winter Care for Ducks

Indian Runner Ducks need special care during the colder months. Remember that domestic birds react to cold conditions just like the wild ducks. The difference lies in the fact that the wild birds are able to migrate to warmer places. On the other hand, the domesticated Runner Ducks will be dependent on you to provide the right environment.

The food essentially remains the same. Wheat, which is ideal for all seasons, forms the main constituent of the diet. If the weather is extremely cold, you can also opt for maize which provides the ducks with the required amount of calories to keep themselves warm.

Ducks must also have constant access to food. You can increase the feeding portions in the summer months as the ducks will require this to thrive and remain healthy in the colder months.

The shelter must be additionally insulated to make sure that the ducks stay warm. This means that the litter inside the shelter must be increased. You can also line the walls of the coop with some insulating material. The trick is to ensure ample ventilation while keeping the duck house warm.

Chapter 5: Acquiring Ducks

Acquiring a duck is more complicated than simply walking in your local pet store and walking out with some new pets. You must ensure that you only purchase healthy ducks, you must be sure to purchase the right ratio of males and females, and you must decide on the best place to shop for the ducks.

1. Selecting a Healthy Pet

When selecting a pet Duck, always strive to acquire the healthiest birds available.

Ill, stressed or injured animals may display any of the following signs:

- Cloudy, swollen or sunken eyes

- Smeared fecal material near their cloaca

- Wings that do not lie flat against the body of the bird, that dangle limply or exhibit any other deformity of lack of function.

- Birds that have visible sores, wounds or areas of missing feathers (do not confuse the scruffy appearance of a molting duck with that of a duck with a health problem).

By contrast, healthy animals will exhibit:

- Strong interactions with other members of the flock

- Strong legs and rapid, purposeful movement

-

- Healthy appetites. Ducks should eat eagerly when fed, and drink water shortly afterwards

2. Social Considerations

It is not advisable to acquire a single Duck, whether male or female. Ducks are very social birds that will imprint on the animals with whom they interact. If they do not have another bird to socialize with, they will imprint on their keeper. While this can make the duck more comfortable in your presence and foster a strong owner-pet bond, the bird will fail to learn how to socialize with other birds.

This is primarily a problem if you decide to add other ducks at a later date. The original bird will not have the capability of existing peacefully in the new society and will be prone to fighting with its cagemates.

Another occasion in which this might cause a problem is if you are forced to place your duck in another home. If, for example, your job requires you to relocate and you are unable to care for your duck, it will be difficult to find a new home for the bird. Having imprinted on you, it will be stressed out being separated from you, and the bird will have to go to a home that does not have any other ducks.

In general, you should purchase at least three or four ducks. Ideally, you will purchase one drake and two or three females, which is an optimum ratio for most pet owners.

It can be difficult to determine the gender of Ducks while they are very young. Accordingly, it makes sense to purchase slightly older ducks that are easily identifiable by gender. Alternatively, breeders and veterinarians can often distinguish between the genders by examining their cloaca (often called the duck's "vent").

3. Buying from Breeders or Hatcheries

Most Ducks are purchased from breeders, and there are many reasons for this. One is that breeders are among the first results to pop up in a typical internet search; pet stores do not often carry ducks year-round, so they do not advertise them as much.

Another reason why breeders are one of the most desirable avenues through which to acquire a duck is sheer selection. Few breeders of Ducks produce only one variety; most breeders have four, five or more variations from which you can choose.

Additionally, breeders are generally better informed about the genetics of the ducks they have available. This is important if you seek to breed your ducks and produce different varieties yourself.

An underappreciated benefit of purchasing a duck from a breeder is that you can be more certain that you obtain unrelated animals. This is important to prevent inbreeding, which can cause the ducks to produce offspring with health problems.

When purchasing animals directly from a breeder, you have the ability to ensure that your animals have been treated well prior to you purchasing them. This is not the case when purchasing birds from retail establishments, as the ducks may have passed through the hands of multiple wholesalers before reaching the retail store.

Finally, the quality of stock offered by breeders is generally superior to the quality available through other avenues.

4. Buying from Retailers

While retail establishments seldom breed Ducks, they may carry hatchlings from time to time, particularly in the spring. Usually Ducks are more common at pet stores, but Ducks can be found at such establishments with ample effort.

The benefits of buying from a retail establishment are numerous. You will usually have your choice among many ducks, you can often hold and interact with them to ascertain their personality and you can see how the birds eat, drink and get along with their cage mates.

Additionally, and perhaps most importantly for new duck keepers, the pet store can provide care information and easy access to some of the supplies you will need. In addition, most pet stores will provide some sort of health guarantee for the ducks.

However, these things come at a price, and ducks will cost much more in a pet store than they will if purchased from a breeder. Nevertheless, typical, pet-quality Ducks are modestly priced. Even if the retailer doubles the price you would pay a breeder, the total difference in price will still be relatively modest.

5. Buying from Individuals

Often, one of the best places to get Ducks is from other pet keepers and duck enthusiasts. Many people acquire Ducks only to become overwhelmed by the numerous chicks they end up with. Often, these people try to sell their surplus, but, finding it a challenging prospect and end up giving away most of the hatchlings.

The problem is that it can be hard to locate such people. The best way to do so is by frequenting online message boards and perusing the local classified sections.

6. The Cost of Ducks

The price you will pay for your Ducks depends on whether you purchase them from a breeder, retailer or individual, as well as the number you purchase, the gender of the ducks and the color varieties selected.

In general, hatchlings that display common colors vary from about $4.00 to $30.00, (£2 to £18) depending on the quantity purchased and the place they were purchased from.

However, the prices for rare color varieties can be astronomical. In 2012, an award-winning drake sold for £1,500 at auction ($2,500) (Mail, 2012).

It is difficult to predict the setup and ongoing costs involved with keeping Ducks. If you already have an enclosed area with a pond, or only plan on providing the ducks with a small children's pool, your startup costs will be fairly low. In contrast, if you plan to fence in a large area, build an elaborate pond or construct stand-alone buildings, the costs can reach into the thousands.

While it may be possible to save some money by purchasing used equipment, such as feeding dishes, watering systems and feather clippers, resist the urge to do so. Usually, the savings are minimal when the potential for disease spread is factored into the equation.

7. Adopting Ducks

The last option available to Duck lovers is adoption. This option is suitable for you if you are looking for a duck that you don't have to shell out too much for. Of course, adoption is also a very noble thing to do as you will be able to provide a rescued duck a loving home.

There are several shelters and rescue homes where you will be able to find Ducks for adoption. When you are looking at adopting a duck, there are some things that you must keep in mind:

- Make sure you check the health of the duck thoroughly. Ducks may have several infections that are dangerous for people, especially salmonella.
- Be prepared for behavioral issues if your duck has had an abusive past.
- Make sure that you are able to afford necessary treatments if required.

When you are sure that you will be able to take the responsibility, you may adopt a loving Duck.

8. Should You Bring Home Ducks or Ducklings?

For new duck owners, this can be a very difficult question. Should you bring home an adult duck? Or should you experience the joy of actually raising a duckling till it is an adult? The answer is quite simple. It entirely depends upon what your real intention of bringing home a duck is.

For those who already have ducks at home, bringing an adult into the group is a safer bet than bringing home a duckling. A group of ducks is less likely to adopt a duckling. However, their chances of getting along with an adult bird are higher. Another reason for bringing home an adult duck is adoption. If you want to give shelter to a wounded or abandoned duck, it is a great and noble ideal. However, with these ducks you must take necessary precautions and quarantine measures.

Of course, a duckling is preferred by many as they want to actually rear the little bird and experience the entire process. You can buy ducklings from animal shelters and also pet stores. If you are already into duck farming, hatching an egg is also a good option to bring home a duckling.

There are several benefits of bringing home an adult duck or a duckling. The only determining factor for you to make this choice is the reason you want to have a pet duck.

Benefits of a Duckling

• You can actually take care of the bird from scratch. From the bedding to the shelter, you can take care of all the elements needed to make the duckling feel at home.
• The temperament of the duckling will be as per your bringing up. You can train them to be highly sociable and gentle when you rear them from the baby years.
• It is easier to make a duckling personable. You can teach

them tricks easily when they are ducklings.

• You can be sure of the health of your duckling. Since it has been with you all along, you can be certain that it is free from parasites and infections.

• If you are looking at raising ducks in a farm alongside other animals, it is advisable to bring home ducklings. They are able to get along with other animals easily when they grow up in the same environment.

Benefits of Ducks

• If you want to your duck to be an addition to an already existing group of pet ducks, an adult duck is a better choice.

• Those who are looking at a lucrative business will benefit by including healthy adult ducks instead of ducklings. There is no need to wait for the duckling to grow into an adult. You can also save on the investments required to raise a duckling.

• You can provide a safer environment to a duck that has been abandoned or orphaned.

• Exhibitors benefit by bringing home well-bred show ducks instead of ducklings. The cost of raising is reduced in this case.

Irrespective of whether you are bringing home an adult duck or a baby duck, you must be highly cautious about the health of the bird. In several cases, even a healthy looking duck might carry salmonella in its feathers and feet. So taking ample quarantine measure is important when you are considering a pet duck.

Chapter 6: Housing Your Pet Duck

There are a variety of different strategies that keepers use to keep their Ducks healthy, safe and comfortable. Each strategy has benefits and drawbacks, meaning that few choices are "right" or "wrong."

Some keepers enjoy providing their ducks with luxurious fields for foraging and expansive ponds for swimming and bathing, while others keep their ducks in concrete-floored pens with drinking water, but no water for swimming.

Some keepers place a premium on ensuring that their ducks cannot escape, nor be reached by predators; whereas others place no pens, fences or roofs over their animals, and simply hope for the best.

Keepers in sub-tropical climates may not find it necessary to provide a shelter for their ducks at night, while keepers in the far north may be forced to provide heated shelters to ensure their Ducks do not fall ill.

Ultimately, the keeper will have to determine the best method for housing his or her ducks. No matter which style of housing you provide your animal, you must address a few common issues. For example:

• The enclosure must allow the ducks adequate space to extend their wings fully and obtain enough exercise.

• The enclosure must allow the ducks enough individual, "personal" space to ensure they remain stress free and to keep pecking and infighting to a minimum.

• The enclosure must have appropriate temperatures for the ducks. While ducks require much higher temperatures when they are young, the optimum temperature for adults is about 55 degrees Fahrenheit. Fully feathered Ducks can tolerate much lower temperatures, but they require shelter to retreat from the winds and heavy rain. The ducks must be able to retreat to the water or shade if the temperatures reach 90 degrees or more.

• The keeper must decide on the desired security level of the duck's area. Ducks do not migrate, but they can fly and may decide to leave. To eliminate the possibility of escape, the duck's area must be enclosed on all sides. Clipping their wings may eliminate them from flying away, but they may still escape on foot or by water.

• Related to the issue of keeping the ducks inside the enclosure, the keeper must decide on the degree to which the enclosure is secure from predators. A roof or net is the only thing that will completely protect the ducks against hawks and owls. Complete security may not even be possible in such cases, as snakes, rats and weasels can penetrate very small holes.

• The enclosed area must be safe for the ducks. Care should be taken to ensure that no plants that are toxic to ducks are in the enclosed space. No sharp or dangerous objects should be in the cage, and the substrate should be suitable for the duck's feet.

• The enclosure must be placed in an area that is suitable for ducks. They should not be housed near food preparation areas, such as backyard barbeque pits and picnic areas. They should not be housed adjacent to areas where dogs or children roam, nor should they be housed immediately next to roads or driveways.

1. Housing for Hatchlings

When you purchase your first group of Ducks, it is best to start with a group of hatchlings. Given that their mother will not be there to keep them warm and safe, you will have to provide these services for them.

Housing the Hatchlings

The best way to house your first Ducks is in an indoor pen or cage. However, the indoor area should not be in a living area. Auxiliary buildings, insulated sheds and detached garages are the best choices.

Hatchlings are among the most vulnerable ducks to predators, and without their mother to protect them they are unlikely to dissuade hungry foxes, hawks or snakes.

Keeping the ducks indoors eliminates the vast majority of predators, allows you to keep a close eye on the little ducklings and is an easy place in which to keep them warm.

The downside of indoor duck maintenance is the mess and smell that will emanate from cages that are not cleaned diligently. Accordingly, you must commit to cleaning the cage every day (perhaps twice per day if the ducks do not enjoy plenty of space). This is not only important for the air quality, but also for the little ducks' health and well-being. It is important to clean both the land area and the water in the cage.

At its most basic, an indoor duck pen consists of an enclosed space, that is outfitted with a heat lamp (or two) and a water container. While it may not be strictly necessary for the water container to be large enough to permit swimming, it will greatly improve the young ducks' quality of life if you provide such opportunities. Regardless, ducks absolutely require clean drinking water throughout the day.

The walls of the enclosed space can be constructed, so that they rest on the floor, or they can be provided via a container. In other words, you may choose to connect several boards to form the walls of the enclosure, or you may choose to use a very large container to form the ducks' enclosure.

The floor of the pen should be covered in soft bedding, such as straw or clean paper (butcher's paper, newsprint, etc.). You can also use bare floors if they are not too cold, but they will require daily cleaning.

Keeping the Hatchlings Warm

It is crucial that the young hatchlings are able to stay warm. If they become chilled, they can become sick and die with alarming rapidity. In the wild, Duck mothers brood their young as necessary during this time; but as most people start with hatchlings (and therefore no mother is present), you will have to ensure the young stay warm.

Young hatchlings have two things working against them that make it hard for them to keep warm. Most obviously, the young birds do not yet have the full suite of feathers that the adults have. These feathers are very effective at insulating the adults, and without them, the young are susceptible to hypothermia.

Secondly, but just as importantly, hatchling ducklings are very small, compared to the adults. This means that the ducklings have a very high amount of surface area, relative to their internal volume, when compared against the surface to volume ratio of adults.

When all other things are equal, the higher the surface to volume ratio of an animal is, the more rapidly it will radiate heat. This means that little ducklings radiate a greater percentage of their internally produced heat per unit of time than the larger adults do.

Fortunately, as they grow, the birds' surface to volume ratio becomes smaller, reducing this problem.

The best way to provide heat for the young birds is to suspend a reflecting-style heat lamp dome over part of their pen. The lamp should be high enough that it will not become wet or covered in dust, paper or straw. This is very important – a drop of cold water can make a hot light bulb explode. Usually, the lamp should be mounted about 18-inches from the floor.

Use a red bulb so that the light does not disturb the ducks during the night. Experiment with different wattages until the temperature under the lamp is about 90 to 95 degrees Fahrenheit. Use a digital thermometer to monitor the temperatures.

When suspending the light bulb, place it so that it only illuminates a portion of the pen. This will allow the ducklings to move out of the light when they attain suitably high temperatures. It is easiest to do this by placing the heat lamp at one end of the enclosure; but you can also accomplish this by suspending the light in the center of the pen, if there is sufficient space outside of the lit area for the ducks to rest. However, this may force the ducklings to split up, so it is best to place it at one end. This creates a natural thermal gradient, which allows the ducks access to a wide range of temperatures.

While you should measure the temperatures of the pen regularly, consider the behavior of the ducks as well. If the ducks are always huddled under the heat lamp, they are not warm enough. In contrast, if they are usually avoiding the heat lamp, the heat lamp may be too warm. Pay attention to what the ducks are telling you, and alter their temperatures accordingly.

Each week, you can lower the temperature of the heat lamp by about 5 degrees, though this is not necessary – if the chicks are too hot, they will simply move from under the lamp. After about two or three weeks, you can stop turning the lamp on during the day. After three to five weeks, the light is not necessary at all, even in cool weather.

As they grow, the ducks will become more and more insulated, their surface to volume ratio will shrink and they will be less susceptible to the cold. Although they are a tropical species, the adults acclimate suitably to sub-freezing temperatures, as long as they are able to find somewhere to dry off and get out of the wind – particularly at night.

Water

Ducks enjoy swimming, but they will not develop serious health problems if they are not able to swim. Make no mistake, swimming accommodations are important to ensure that your duck lives a full and enriched life; however, they will not die for lack of swimming water.

However, without fresh water for drinking, ducks will quickly become ill. Death can follow in as little as 24 to 48 hours with no water.

Accordingly, you must make sure that young ducklings always have access to fresh drinking water. The best way to provide this is via a small, shallow dish or with a commercially produced duck waterer.

Dishes can be made from glass, plastic or ceramic, but avoid galvanized steel with ducks. When offering water for young ducklings it is important to keep the dish shallow, as baby ducks can drown very easily.

Nipple style water dispensers also work well for ducks, although you may need to show them that the nipples release water.

This water must be kept very clean to prevent the ducks from getting sick. Unfortunately, the ducks often seem determined to make the biggest mess possible. You will have to change the water every day and clean out the dish with soap and water. You can help keep the water cleaner by providing more than one water dish, which will tend to spread the mess over more water.

Once the birds have reached three to five weeks of age, you can start allowing them to swim in very shallow pools. Keep the water less than ½ inch deep until the young ducklings are strong swimmers. Always be sure that the ducks can get into and out of the water very easily.

Over the next several weeks, you can begin transitioning the ducks to their long-term housing protocols. For example, if you plan to move the ducks to an outdoor pond when they mature, you can begin taking them for brief, supervised outings so that they can gradually become accustomed to their future home.

Alternatively, if you plan to herd the ducks, you will need to begin familiarizing them with the daily procedure, while supervising them whenever they are outside.

2. Long Term Housing

By the time your Ducks are about 12 weeks old, you can treat them as adults. There are several different basic housing options, and each has a nearly infinite capacity for customization.

Water for Swimming?

While Ducks certainly need copious amounts of clean water for drinking, they do not require swimming water for survival. It is true that Ducks are not as aquatic as Duck-derived breeds, but they appreciate a swimming area that affords them the chance to bathe, swim and forage.

Tens of millions of Ducks are produced each year in commercial operations, and most of these do not provide swimming water for their livestock. However, the goals and ethos of a commercial duck production facility are different from those of a pet owner. A pet owner should always seek to provide their companions with the highest quality of life possible.

If the prospect of providing and maintaining swimming water for the animals is not palatable, perhaps waterfowl are not an ideal pet for you.

With that said, offering your pets swimming water for several hours, two or three times a week may be a sufficient compromise. In some respects, this approach may even be better for the ducks' long-term well-being.

Given a small flock of three or four Ducks, a large child's plastic wading pool may be large enough to give the birds the exercise they need. Such a swimming pool can be emptied, cleaned and re-filled between uses to ensure clean water. The lack of swimming water will also prevent a great deal of the mess that the ducks will create as they drag water all over the enclosure, creating mud.

Simplest Enclosure Possible

Often, the best way to house ducks – particularly for new keepers – is the simplest way possible. This means eliminating any unnecessary components of the enclosure and providing only the things that the ducks require to remain healthy and happy.

To accomplish this, provide your Ducks with a small, enclosed, outdoor pen with a large, permanent water container. A small child's swimming pool or stock tank can be added to the enclosed space to provide swimming opportunities. In the interest of simplicity, it is best to fill the pool periodically, rather than leaving it full all of the time. Be sure to flip the pool upside down when not in use to prevent the ducks from falling in and injuring themselves.

In principle, such a pen features several wooden posts and some material to form the pen's walls (and roof, if so desired). It is possible to use existing structures as a portion of the enclosure. For example, if the pen is constructed next to a building, one of the building's exterior walls can serve as one of the enclosure's walls.

Many different materials can be used to make the enclosure's walls. Chicken-wire and similar metal mesh products are popular choices. When possible, plastic-coated wires should be used, as they are less likely to cause injury.

Alternatively, the walls of the pen can be made from corrugated plastic panels, wood that has been sealed for outdoor use, or cement. Poured cement walls are hard to beat in terms of durability, but building such walls is a significant undertaking.

Be sure that the gaps in the fence are either small enough to prevent the ducks from poking their heads through the holes at all or large enough that they can poke their heads through and retract them without becoming stuck. Always ensure that there are no exposed sharp edges or rough surfaces when attaching the metal material to the supports.

While such pens need not be expansive, it must be large enough to allow the ducks enough space for exercise and personal space. Two to four ducks will live happily in a pen with approximately 100 square feet (9.36 square meters) of space.

The simplest floors to maintain are made of smooth concrete. By pouring the floor at a gentle slope, the floor can be hosed down and kept clean with ease. However, pouring a concrete floor is a significant undertaking that may be beyond the skill set or budget for one keeping a few pet ducks.

If concrete floors are impractical, several other choices are possible. Wood shavings or mulch make a suitable ground cover, although they will require frequent replacement. Additionally, you must be sure that the wood chips are not sharp or too rough, as they may injure your ducks' delicate feet.

Grass, clover or similar ground covers are suitable, although it is more difficult to keep this area clean. The duck's droppings will biodegrade over time, but in a small enclosure, their waste will build up more quickly than it will degrade. The only viable approach for small, grass-floored pens is to remove droppings manually, once or twice per week.

In addition, the enclosure will require some type of shelter or roost in which the ducks can sleep and retreat from inclement weather.

A variety of different shelters are possible, from elaborate, custom built shelters, made from wood and screws, to simple, plastic dog houses. The shelter must be large enough for the ducks to extend their wings and have enough personal space to avoid causing stress and infighting – especially if the ducks are forced to remain in the shelter overnight.

Raised Pens

Instead of constructing a pen directly on the ground, it is possible to build a raised pen for your Ducks. Raising the pen off the ground entails a great deal more effort in terms of designing and constructing the enclosure, but the benefits of a raised pen are substantial.

Usually, such pens are constructed by building a wooden frame, and then enclosing the area as with a standard pen, by using some type of metal mesh. By raising the cage off the ground, the ducks' droppings will pass through the floor of the pen onto the ground below. While the keeper will still be forced to contend with the copious droppings, they will not remain in contact with the ducks. This helps to ensure that the ducks stay healthy and clean. In addition, spilled drinking or swimming water will not saturate the ground, causing a muddy mess inside the cage.

Additionally, because such pens are elevated, it is possible to plumb a swimming pool, which will allow easy filling and draining. By cutting a hole in the bottom of a small stock tank or children's wading pool, you can attach PVC fittings and pipes that will serve as a drain. If the piping is sized to fit a hose, the soiled water can be drained and used to water lawns or ornamental plants in other parts of the yard.

It is generally easy to mount the swimming pool flush with the floor by cutting a hole in a section of the mesh floor, and constructing a frame of wood around the hole to support the lip or rim of the pool.

Raised pens require a shelter as well. The easiest way to provide one is by covering the roof and three walls of one end of the cage to create a covered alcove. In particularly cold climates, it may be advisable to use a solid floor for the cage to reduce drafts that come up through the floor.

One of the greatest benefits of raised pens is that it is easy to fill and drain the swimming pool. Additionally, raised pens do not become muddy, and keep your ducks cleaner than pens built on the ground. Finally – and most importantly for some keepers – raised pens are very secure from many predators. However, these benefits are offset to some degree by the cost and labor involved in constructing a pen suitably sized for such large ducks.

While many keepers – particularly small-scale breeders – use raised pens for young ducks, relatively few keepers use raised pens for adult Ducks. This is due in part to the ducks' large size. At a minimum, the pen should have approximately 100 square feet (9.36 square meters) of space, and be a minimum of 30 to 36 inches ((75 to 100 centimeters) high.

Such large structures may not be permissible in some residential areas, or they may require expensive construction permits to erect. Additionally, some may consider them to be an eyesore unless constructed in such a way to be aesthetically pleasing.

Free Range

If you are blessed to have a large amount of land, you may elect to keep your ducks in a free-range manner. To do so, the ducks are allowed to roam as they wish, although it is advisable to use a fence around the perimeter of the property to prevent the ducks from wandering off.

This is a very rewarding way of housing your ducks, but it requires a large space, considerable effort to "duck-proof" the area and is the least secure method for housing your beloved pets.

When keeping your ducks out in the open, hawks and owls are an ever-present threat to your pets, even if a perimeter fence excludes dogs, coyotes and foxes.

The relative risk to adult Ducks is modest, but young ducklings are very vulnerable to hawks and owls. There are ways to reduce the risk further, such as employing the services of a guard or herding dog. While far from infallible, few birds of prey will venture too close to a large canine.

Free range ducks must have a suitable enclosure for sleeping and avoiding bad weather and predators.

Often, free-range housing is used to take advantage of an existing pond or water feature. This provides the ducks with a wonderful resource for swimming, bathing, escaping terrestrial predators and foraging. Additionally, if of sufficient size, such naturally occurring ponds are unlikely to become polluted from two to four ducks. For larger flocks, care must be taken to ensure the ducks' droppings do not overwhelm the pond's flora and fauna.

Free range keeping of Ducks should only be conducted if you own or have rights to the entire area to which they have access. In other words, do not attempt to keep Ducks in a free-range manner in a large reservoir that connects to different properties. Not only could the ducks be injured by pets or unsupervised children, but your neighbors may not appreciate your pets' droppings on their manicured lawns.

Keeping your Ducks in a free range system means that they may fly away if their wings have not been pinioned or clipped. However, if the ducks have plentiful food, water and shelter, they are unlikely to leave the area.

Herding

Many keepers employ a modified free-range technique. Called "herding," the technique is largely similar to free range keeping, but the ducks are herded into a dedicated sleeping shelter at night. Once inside their sleeping quarters, the ducks are locked in securely. The next morning, the ducks are herded back to their activity area.

Herding drastically reduces the chances of predation at night, yet still allows the ducks daily access to natural forage and swimming opportunities. Additionally, by having two different activity zones for the ducks (the daytime activity area and the sleeping quarters); you can tend to one while the ducks are in the other. This is easier for the keeper, and less stressful for the kept.

Grass

In the wilderness, ducks are usually found near ponds and brooks that have long grass growing around them. This serves two purposes. First, the ducks are able to hide between the long blades of grass to protect themselves from predators. Second, the area between the grass provides the ideal location for foraging. This is where the duck's favorite snacks are available easily.

Likewise, even when they are domesticated or bred, ducks maintain the same attachment to grass. It is recommended that you grow grass around the waterers and the ponds that you have created for your ducks. Allow the blades to grow as long as possible. Ideally, the grass should grow taller than the Indian Runners. This will help them hide and forage just as they would in the wild.

Shades and Trees

Landscaping is an important part of owning ducks. In order to give your ducks the perfect free raging experience, you must make sure that they feel as close to nature as possible.

One thing that ducks strive for is shade. They are easily harmed by excessive sun exposure. So, having trees and bushes will provide them with the shade that they need. If you do not have room for trees in your backyard, you can even plant bushes that grow tall and thick. You will see your Indian Runners resting in their shade during the hot summer months.

Another advantage of having plenty of trees and bushes is that they will attract bugs and insects. These bugs make great food for your ducks. Foraging for bugs and snacking on them also gives your Runners something to do. When you are choosing plants, trees or even shrubs to landscape the area where you keep your ducks, you must be very careful. Some varieties can be extremely toxic for ducks. So, before you landscape you yard, do your research and understand what trees and shrubs work best with ducks.

Bedding

The best option for bedding, especially for ducklings is rye straw. Remember, the bedding that you choose must provide ample cushioning and must also turn into a comfortable nest if you do not have a separate nest altogether. There are several other materials that make comfortable and warm bedding for ducks. Some common choices are peanut hulls, crushed corncobs, wood shavings and even sawdust. You must make sure that the shavings are not from treated wood or from cedar trees.

The bedding material that you choose must be mold resistant as ducks will bring in moisture every time they come back after a swim.

Straw is considered a very poor bedding option, especially for ducklings. Within a few minutes of hatching, ducklings will start to forge. Anything that looks worm-like, will be eaten. So, ducks and ducklings usually choke on straw. If you are, however, insistent on using straw, make sure that you choose a variety that is larger. Straw must be replaced as soon as it becomes even slightly moist.

Another important factor to remember whole choosing bedding for your ducks is the footing. If you use slippery material like newspapers, you are likely to damage the legs of the ducks. They develop a condition called 'sprawled legs' when they are forced in an environment where they do not have ample footing.

You can try different materials until you find one that your ducks like the best. All you need to ensure is that the bedding is soft, warm and completely mold resistant.

Making a Pond

For those who are planning to have ducks in their backyard, a duck pond would be a beautiful addition to the landscape. In addition to being a great place for your ducks to go for a swim and just hang out with their group, the duck pond also acts like a great aesthetic piece in your garden or backyard.

Materials you will need

Setting up the perfect pond is quite the struggle. It involves a lot of labor and can be slightly expensive if you want it to last longer. Quite frankly, for the amount of effort that you would put into engineering a duck pond, you might as well make that investment.

For the basic structure, polythene landfill liner works best. It is durable and is resistant to the roots of trees and plants. You may also choose butyl but it is not half as robust as polythene. The edges of the pond must be secured with underlay made from felt before you actually lower it in to the ground. To make the pond appear natural, burying it in gravel or even riddled soil works well. It is also useful in protecting the pond from damage caused by UV rays.

How big should the pond be?

If your pond is too shallow or too small, your runner ducks will not be able to have a great time in it. With a smaller pond, there is also a risk of temperature fluctuations and easy soiling because of the little volume of water. This causes rapid growth of algae and weed that are damaging to the health of your runner duck. In a large pond, there is no need to pump in algicide either.

Ideally, a good duck pond should be at least 12 inches wide and 24 inches deep. Of course, this changes if the number of ducks is more.

Plants in the Pond

Plants are a must in a pond that is being designed for ducks. They make the perfect spaces for the ducks to forage around and look for food. They also give the ducks a sense of security because, instinctively, ducks love to hide between water plants.

Oxygenating plants are a must for a duck pond. They will not allow algae to thrive in the water. You see, algae only flourish in anaerobic conditions, i.e, in the lack of oxygen. These plants add oxygen to the water making it impossible for algae to grow.

It is better to allow the plants that you add to the pond to grow fully before the ducks are given access to the pond. In a duck pond, it is never a good idea to have plants like lotus and water lily which have floating leaves. These plants are unable to withstand the bashing around that ducks love to do. So, it is best to plant saplings that are marginal. They will border the pond and will not have to encounter the nipping and splashing of the ducks.

Some of the best suited plants are marsh marigold, shuttlecock fern, mares tail and pickerel weed. Some varieties of marginal plants are not exactly robust. However, they will be able to survive with the ducks. The advantage of most of these marginal plants is that they will self seed. So once they are fully grown, you need not really worry about rotating the plants or even planting new saplings.

You must always take great care while purchasing plants for your pond. If you buy weak plants, the dabbling of your ducks will only leave a big mess around the pond. The ideal plants are those that have fibrous stems and roots. You can simply plant these saplings in the soil or gravel around the pond and just allow them to grow thereafter.

Why ducks love ponds

There are several waterfowl experts who believe that swimming water is not really a necessity for runner ducks. Of course, there are several flocks where the older birds will merely dip their beaks in to the water once in a while. However, the truth is that if there is good, clean water available, your runners will love it. The younger birds and the birds that are about to breed are benefitted by a good pond the most.

Remember that the slugs and the greens available at the pond will provide the best source of minerals for the younger ducks.

When you just introduce a flock to the pond, especially if they are ducklings, make sure that they are supervised throughout their time in the water. The water must also be replaced on a regular basis to ensure that it does not cause infections and health issues. A still water body like a pond does get soiled very easily. If it is left dirty, it becomes the ideal breeding ground for mosquitoes undesirable pests.

Safety measures

When you have a pond out in the open for your ducks, it is quite obvious that there are several external factors that can cause damage to your beloved ducks. So, you must take some precautions and safety measure before allowing the ducks to access the pond:

- **Keep Other Wildlife away:** A pond that is out in the open may also be accessed by other wildlife. If you have seen the presence of harmless animals and birds around the pond, you need not worry. However, the presence of predators means that you must keep the possible entry points closed. Ensure that invaders are unable to enter your home in the first place.

- **Make the access easy:** If the pond is hard to get in and out of, your duck might suffer serious leg injuries. Make sure that you define the access points of the pond with gentle slopes. The ducks will be able to simple slide in and then waddle out when they want to.

- **Select the plants carefully:** Although there are several plants that are
robust enough to survive the dabbling and the foraging of these ducks, they may not be the ideal additions to your duck pond. For instance, a common pond marginal plant, the Parrot's Tail, tends to grow quite long. This plant might get entangled with the feet or body of the duck making it difficult for it to swim. Ducks are delicate creature and may also suffer from sprains and fractures in an attempt to free themselves from the tangles of such plants.

- **Separate the groups of ducks:** If you have ducks and ducklings in your backyard, it is a good idea to keep them from entering the pond at the same time. There have been several instances where adult drakes have held ducklings underwater and drowned them. The reason for this type of behavior is unknown. However, just keeping the ducks and ducklings away from each other is a safer option.

- **Provide Shade:** It is a common belief among duck owners that the presence of water is good enough to keep the ducks comfortable and cool. However, ducks are easily prone to sunburns. Since they might choose to spend a good amount of time in the pond, providing them with ample shade is a great idea. You can build a pond under the shade of a tree if possible. If that is not an option, artificial structures like sheets and roofs can be put up to protect the birds.

If a pond is not a possibility, even kiddie pools work really well with ducks. A pond, however, adds to the charm and appeal of having waterfowl in your little backyard.

74

Adapting an Existing Pond

Of course, it is easier to provide a pond for your ducks if you already have one on your land. However, depending on the prior use of the pond, it may not be ready for ducks.

It is important to ensure that the pond does not have any submerged objects that may injure or ensnare the birds. This includes sunken boats, trash, construction materials and lost fishing lures or string. Fishing line and tackle is an especially dangerous item to have in duck ponds. The ducks often eat lead weights, as they look similar to nuts or seeds. This can cause them to develop lead poisoning. Fishing line can ensnare them badly enough that they never break free. If the fishing line is under the water, it may also cause the ducks to drown.

Additionally, the pond must be easy for the ducks to enter and exit. The best option is to construct a gently sloping beach if one does not already exist. The ducks may be able to scale shores successfully if they are built from riprap or large boulders, but the rough surfaces may abrade the ducks' delicate feet. Additionally, riprap provides excellent places for predators, such as snakes and minks, to hide.

The pond will likely support more forage if it has abundant plant life. While you should be able to access all portions of the pond, some portions of the pond-land interface should have ample vegetation on the land and in the water.

You can stock the pond with turtles, fish and frogs if you wish, but their impact on the water chemistry must be taken into account. In general, the more animals that are present, the more vegetation is necessary. The vegetation will use much of the ammonia produced by the animals, and oxygenate the water.

Ponds that are in direct sunlight for the bulk of the day will tend to suffer from higher algae blooms and an increased rate of evaporation. However, ponds that receive direct sunlight are less likely to freeze than shaded ponds are.

Depending on the flora and fauna you intend to stock the pond with, the depth of the water will have to account for local weather conditions. For example, a pond in the southern United States may not be at risk of freezing, so great depth is not necessary to prevent fish, turtles or frogs from dying off in the winter. In contrast, a pond in western Canada must be very deep to prevent killing fish or frogs in the winter.

For those living in cold climates, it may not be feasible to provide the ducks with swimming water year-round. This will not harm their health, but they must be given regular access to drinking water.

Predator-Proof Checklist

Many different animals view your beloved pets as a tempting and tasty snack. While it is very difficult to eliminate this possibility, most keepers are keen to reduce these odds as much as possible. Ultimately, the keeper will have to decide the level of risk they are willing to take on behalf of their birds.

Hatchling Ducks are at the greatest risk to predators. Their small size means that a greater number of animals are capable of consuming them and their inexperience makes them less prepared to avoid predators. Hatchling and juvenile Ducks are at risk of the following predators:

Large snakes	Dingoes
Hawks	Falcons
Owls	Raccoons
Ravens	Opossums
Crows	Foxes
Magpies	Coyotes
Kestrels	Bobcats

Weasels	Wolverines
Minks	Ferrets / pole cats
Otters	Domestic Dogs
Herons and other large wading birds	Domestic Cats
	Bears
Large turtles	Large predatory fish
Crocodilians	Large amphibians, particularly frogs
Skunks	
Rats	
Badgers	

Additionally, keepers who reside in tropical regions must contend with large lizards, primates and other ground-based predators, such as mongooses.

By virtue of their large size, adult Ducks are not at risk of many of the predators that can consume young ducks. Additionally, their life experience helps them to avoid many predators by swimming or flying away. However, the adults are still at risk of:

Large Hawks	Wolverines
Large Owls	Badgers
Foxes	Crocodilians
Coyotes	Bobcats
Dingoes	Bears
Domestic Dogs	Raccoons
Domestic Cats	

Additionally, in areas where such predators exist, very large snakes, lizards, primates or cats may also prey upon ducks.

When constructing your outdoor pen, consider the following questions:

- Are the ducks protected from untrustworthy and unknown canines?

- Are the ducks protected from domestic or feral cats, raccoons, opossums, weasels and other climbing and digging predators?

- Are the ducks protected from birds of prey? This is important during the day (hawks) and at night (owls).

- Are the ducks protected from small animals, such as rats and snakes?

- Are the ducks protected from malevolent Homo sapiens?

- Are the ducks protected from aquatic predators, such as large fish, turtles and crocodilians?

You can also experiment with anti-predator devices, as long as they do not frighten the ducks. For example, a scarecrow may dissuade crows and small hawks. Predator decoys, such as plastic owls, may discourage rats, snakes and other small animals from hunting your young ducks.

Decoys that move – such as when they are blown by the wind – are more effective than completely stationary ones. If this is not possible, consider moving the decoy regularly. Other techniques, such as sprinkler systems and noise-making devices may dissuade terrestrial predators, such as foxes and dogs.

Do not use commercial chemical repellants to keep predators away from your ducks. Such chemicals rarely work, and often have harmful components. Remember that your ducks' pond is at the bottom of your local watershed, and anything that is poured on the surrounding land will usually wash into the water.

Ultrasonic noise producers and similar devices should be avoided as well. They may irritate your ducks and keep much of their insect prey from venturing into the area.

Some duck keepers place predator traps along the periphery of the property in hopes of reducing the local population. Usually, this is an exercise in futility, as it is very difficult to consistently trap predators.

Even if you manage to catch one or two predators, the other ones in the area are just as likely to stay close by, and devour your precious ducklings at a later date. Many intelligent predators – especially dogs, foxes and coyotes – learn to recognize and avoid traps very quickly.

Traps can be dangerous to ducks and humans as well as predators, so you must weigh the potential protective value of the traps versus the potential for injuring one of your ducks or children. Additionally, if you are successful in trapping the predator, you will be faced with an injured, frightened animal that must be humanely euthanized. Such procedures exceed the capabilities and skill of casual duck owners.

Trapping regulations vary widely from one location to the next, so be sure to check with your local officials to avoid conflicting with the law.

Depending upon the type of predator that you are dealing with, you may take necessary precautions. For instance, if you have to deal with a Bobcat that is threatening the safety of your ducks, you can also bring home a dog that will be able to safeguard your ducks.

If you have had attacks during the day, you may also hire someone to supervise the space for a while. When predators are aware of the supervision, they will strike less often.

The biggest mistake that you can make with predators is providing them with space to hide. If there are large sacks or cans, you must get rid of them immediately. Predators like coyotes love to hide watch and then attack. If their hiding spaces are eliminated, even the attacks will reduce significantly.

The other important precaution for duck owners is to ensure that there is no garbage that is out in the open. This prevents predators such as raccoons that come in primarily to get some food. Then, they end up attacking your precious pets.

If you feel like none of your precautions are working, you may also contact your Local Environment Council. They will be able to provide you with the right methods of controlling the most prolific predators.

Chapter 7: Feeding Your Pet Duck

Feeding your duck properly is more complicated than simply tossing a few pieces of bread into their pen each day. You must ensure that you offer them the right types of food, a diverse variety of food and that you offer it at the proper frequency.

1. Food

Ideally, pet Ducks have the opportunity to eat several different types of food. In addition to commercially produced food and the occasional table scrap, Ducks should always have the ability to consume natural forage as well.

Natural Forage

One of the most important aspects for both keeping your pets healthy and maximizing the benefits they offer is ensuring that they forage for natural foods. Wild and range-reared Ducks consume an amazing amount of insects, spiders, tick, slugs and snails. These foods are an important – and free – component of the species' diet. Some farmers keep a flock of Ducks simply for their pest control contributions.

In northern latitudes, Ducks may be more inclined to consume insects in the afternoon, once the land has warmed sufficiently. Ducks living in warmer climates may forage for insects earlier in the day.

In addition to insects and other invertebrates, Ducks also consume a large amount of grass and herbaceous vegetation. If the size of the flock is in balance with the size of the area, the ducks can keep a lawn reasonably well trimmed. Ducks also consume fruits, whether they find them on the ground or attached to the plant.

Because they may harm plants in pursuit of their creepy-crawly prey, some keepers find it necessary to confine the ducks' activities or protect sensitive plants with fencing.

Commercially Prepared Foods

Commercially prepared duck chow should form the bulk of your ducks' diet. In an ideal scenario, your ducks would obtain all of their food by foraging, but this may lead them to stray from your yard if they are not completely contained or if they have not had their wings clipped or pinioned.

Accordingly, the best idea for most keepers is to provide enough commercial food to keep the ducks well fed and happy to hang around, but not so much that they lose interest in foraging.

Creating food for ducks and other poultry is a multi-billion dollar industry. Accordingly, a wide variety of feed is available, each tailored to a different type and age of duck. Additionally, these foods are often specifically designed for birds that are being raised for meat, egg production or as pets.

In general, growing chicks require a significant portion of protein in their diet to fuel the construction of new body tissues. As they grow, their protein needs gradually decline.

Some duck breeders feed their ducks high-protein foods until they mature and begin to lay. In some cases, this food may be composed of up to 28 percent protein.

Egg-laying females require extra calcium to produce eggshells. Many foods for laying hens contain up to 20 percent protein.

Most breeders recommend switching from a high-protein "starter" food to a "breeder" food, with lower protein, at about three to five weeks of age.

It is important that you do not offer chicken food to ducks. Many chicken foods contain medication that will make your Ducks sick. Some duck keepers and breeders seek to mix their own feeds. This is often necessary if you cannot find the correct protein percentage for your ducks.

If you are not sure which type of food to offer your Ducks, consult your veterinarian. Alternatively, the breeder from whom you purchased the birds may be able to suggest the proper food for your pets.

Other Dietary Items

It is usually acceptable to offer your Ducks table scraps on occasion. Avoid greasy, salty foods.

Fruits

Blackberries

Blueberries

Raspberries

Cranberries

Boysenberries

Loganberries

Pear (sliced or cubed)

Squash (sliced or cubed)

Pumpkin (cubed)

Apple (sliced of cubed)

Papaya (sliced of cubed)

Grapes (sliced)

Pineapple (cubed)

Water melon (cubed)

Sweet peppers (sliced)

Eggplant (cubed)

Peaches (sliced or cubed)

Cucumber (sliced or cubed)

Figs (sliced)

Persimmons (sliced)

Cantaloupe (cubed)

Vegetables

Collard greens (cut)	Cabbage (cut)
Spinach (only in moderation)	Cauliflower (cut into small pieces)
Romaine lettuce (cut)	
Radicchio (cut)	Asparagus (cut)
Carrots (shredded or cubed)	Kale (cut)
Broccoli (cut into small pieces)	Beets (cut)
	Most sprouts

Grains, Legumes and Seeds

Cracked corn	Cooked snow peas (cut)
Popcorn	Cooked lima beans
Wheat	Cooked black beans
Barley	Cooked pinto beans
Oats	Sunflower seeds
Rice	Safflower seeds
Milo	Sesame seeds
Peas	Pumpkin seeds
Cooked green beans (cut)	Mixed bird seed (no Peanuts)

Many plants that grow in your yard are acceptable food for Ducks. Always be sure that toxic chemicals, such as fertilizers, pesticides or insecticides, are not used in areas where your ducks feed.

Dandelion	Bermuda grass
Clover	Winter rye grass

Fescue grass	Wintergrass
Centipede grass	Wheat grass
Zoysia grass	Crab grass
Rye grass	Tall oat grass
Blue grass	Orchard grass
Kikuyu grass	Grape leaves
Blue Grama grass	
Dallas grass	

Additionally, there are a variety of live animals that you can supplement your ducks' diet with.

Crickets	Moths
Mealworms	Leaches
Superworms	Grasshoppers
Wax worms	Roaches
Silk worms	Guppies
Earthworms	Minnows
Nightcrawlers	Shad
Red Wigglers	Goldfish

2. Frequency

Ducks need to eat every day. Ideally, your ducks will consume a varied diet, including commercially produced food, fruits and vegetables, and worms and other small feeders you provide. Additionally, your Ducks should consume a large amount of wild grasses, insects and other items as well.

Many keepers help encourage their Ducks to forage by providing them with commercial food in the afternoons. Others choose to simply feed their ducks each day, and allow them to eat the commercial diet when they choose.

Others leave food out at all times. While this is an acceptable strategy, you must be sure to keep the feeding containers clean. Do not simply pour new commercial food on top of the uneaten food in the food dish.

Always be sure that the ducks have access to water whenever food is present. Otherwise, the ducks could have trouble swallowing their food and they may choke.

3. Things to Avoid

Unless directed by your veterinarian, avoid medicated duck feeds. Improper use of such foods can cause lameness or death.

Do not feed your ducks bread. While bread is not toxic to birds, it is a very poor food source. Packed with sugar and calories, but very little else, bread takes up a lot of room in the ducks' digestive tract, without offering any substantial nutrition.

Additionally, ducks love to eat bread, and will often do so while forsaking all other foods. Bread can take up space in the ducks' esophagus or gizzard, potentially blocking them and causing further problems.

Spinach and other vegetables that are high in oxalic acids are not toxic to ducks, but they should only be fed in moderation. Such vegetables bind with the calcium in the ducks' diets, leading to deficiencies – this is especially problematic for laying females.

Onions are toxic to birds. Garlic, shallots and chives should also be avoided as they are similar and may cause serious health problems. Prolonged exposure to onions can cause birds to develop a condition known as hemolytic anemia.

Chocolate is toxic to many animals, including Ducks. If the birds eat chocolate, it can cause them to experience significant digestive disorders. Serious cases involving chocolate poisoning can cause nervous system problems, convulsions and death.

Avocados are incredibly toxic to birds. All parts of the plant can cause fatal heart problems for your ducks.

Avoid feeding your ducks processed foods. This includes canned vegetables and processed carbohydrates. Such foods are invariably high in salts, fats and sugars. Although they are not technically toxic, these substances can cause serious health problems for your ducks in surprisingly small quantities.

Nuts are swallowed whole by ducks, and if too many are consumed, they can fill the esophagus, causing digestive problems. While some wild ducks routinely eat acorns, it is best to err on the side of caution. Additionally, most nuts have a high fat content, which is not ideal for the ducks.

Citrus fruits are simply too acidic for ducks. Avoid oranges, lemons, limes and grapefruit.

While unsalted and unbuttered popcorn does not represent a health hazard from a nutritional standpoint, the shape and texture of the food can cause problems. Ducks often get the popcorn stuck in their throat, where it can cause abrasions and wounds.

Potentially Toxic Plants

Little research has been performed to determine which plants, if any, are toxic to ducks. In general, Ducks are not likely to experience health problems from eating toxic plants. Whether this is due to natural immunity or aversion to toxic species remains unknown.

It is wise to inspect the area in which the ducks will spend time and learn which plants are in the area. A small field guide to the herbaceous plants in your area should help you identify any unknown species. Your local agricultural extension office is also a valuable resource for learning about local plants.

The following chart contains many of the plants that either are known to be toxic to ducks, or are known to be toxic to other animals, such as cat and dogs:

Common Name	Scientific Name
Amaryllis	*Amaryllis belladonna*
Anemone	*Anemone* sp.
Anthurium	*Anthurium* sp.
Asparagus Fern	*Asparagus sprengerii*
Arrowhead Vine	*Syngonium podophyllum*
Atamasco Lily	*Zephyranthes* sp.
Azalea	*Rhododendron sp.*
Autumn Crocus	*Colchicum autumnale*
Avocado	*Persean Americana*
Baneberry	*Actaea* sp.
Begonia	*Begonia* sp.
Bird of Paradise	*Poinciana gilliesii*
Black Cherry	*Prunus serotina*
Black Locust	*Robinia pseudoacacia*
Black Nightshade	*Solanum nigrum*
Black Snakeroot	*Zigadenus* sp.
Bleeding Heart	*Dicentra spectabilis*
Bloodroot	*Sanguinaria canadensis*

Boxwood	*Buxus* sp
Boston Ivy	*Parthenocissus tricuspidata*
Buttercup	*Ranunculus* sp.
Butterfly Weed	*Asclepias* sp.
Caladium	*Caladium* sp.
Calla Lily	*Zantedeschia* sp.
Candytuft	*Iberis* sp.
Cardinal Flower	*Lobelia cardinalis*
Carolina Jasmine	*Gelsemium sempervirens*
Castor Beans	*Ricinus communis*
Cherry Laurel	*Prunus caroliniana*
Chinaberry	*Melia azedarach*
Christmas Rose	*Helleborus niger*
Clematis	*Clematis* sp.
Coriander	*Coriandrum sativum*
Corn Cockle	*Agrostemma githago*
Cowslip	*Caltha palustris*
Daffodil	*Narcissus* sp.
Delphinium	*Delphinium* sp.
Elderberry	*Sambucus* sp.
English Ivy	*Hedera helix*
Four O'clock	*Mirabilis jalapa*

Foxglove	*Digitalis purpurea*
Giant Elephant Ear	*Alocasia sp.*
Gloriosa Lily	*Glonosa superba*
Golden Chain Tree	*Labunum anagryroides*
Goldenseal	*Hydrastis canadensis*
Henbane	*Hyoscyamus niger*
Holly	*Ilex sp.*
Horse Chestnut	*Aesculus sp.*
Hyacinth	*Hyacinthus orientalis*
Hydrangeas	*Hydrangea sp.*
Ivy (Common / English)	*Hedera helix*
Irises	*Iris sp.*
Jack-In-The-Pulpit	*Arisaemia triphyllum*
Jerusalem Cherry	*Solanum pseudocapsicum*
Junipers / Red Cedars	*Juniperus sp.*
Lilly of the Nile	*Agapanthus africanus*
Lilly of the Valley	*Convallaria sp.*
Lobelia	*Lobelia sp.*
Lucky Nut	*Thevetia peruviana*
Lupine	*Lupinus sp.*
Marijuana	*Cannabis sp.*
Meadow Buttercup	*Ranunculus acris*

Milkweed	*Asclepias* sp.
Mistletoe	*Viscum* sp.
Mock Orange	*Philadelphus* sp.
Mountain Laurel	*Kalmia latifolia*
Mourning Glory	Family *Convolvulaceae*
Nandina	*Nandinaa domestica*
Nightshades	*Solanum* sp.
Parsley	*Petroselinum crispum*
Periwinkle	*Vinca minor* and *V. major*
Philodendron	*Philodendron* sp.
Pittosporum	*Pittosporum* sp.
Poinsettia	*Euphorbia pulcherrima*
Potato Plants	*Solanum tuberosum*
Pothos	*Pothos* sp.
Primrose	*Primula* sp.
Privet	*Ligustrum* sp.
Rapeseed	*Brassica napus*
Rhubarb (leaves)	*Rheum rhabarbarum*
Rosary Bean	*Abrus precatarius*
Schefflera	*Schefflera* sp.
Shasta Daisy	*Chrysanthemum maximum*
Sorghum	*Sorghum* sp.

Spider Mum	*Chrysanthemum morifolium*
Split Leaf Philodendron	*Monstera deliciosa*
Spring Adonis	*Adonis vernalis*
St. John's Wort	*Hypericum perforatum*
Strawberry Bush	*Euonymous* sp.
Tobacco	*Nicotiana* sp.
Trumpet Flower	*Solandra* sp.
Umbrella Tree	*Schefflera actinophylla*
Water Hemlock	*Cicuta maculata*
Weeping Yew	*Taxus* sp.
Wisteria	*Wisteria* sp.

Source: www.allthedirtongardening.com

This list is not exhaustive. If you are concerned about plant species that are not on this list, check with your local poison control center or veterinarian for more information.

Grit

When discussing ducks, the term grit refers to fine sand and small rocks that partially fill the duck's gizzard. This material functions similarly to the teeth of other animals. The gizzard – technically called the ventriculus - is a muscular organ that helps to digest their food. To improve the performance of the organ, ducks swallow grit and then carry it in their gizzard.

The gizzard is a very interesting organ, and it is capable of changing its size in response to the food the duck is eating. For example, ducks that routinely consume foods hard to digest usually exhibit enlarged gizzards. Those that consume softer plants and fruits have more modestly sized gizzards.

You must provide some type of grit for your ducks so that they can digest their food properly. If your ducks are kept outdoors and have access to a variety of sands and mud, they will find their own grit. However, if they are kept in concrete-floored pens, or are otherwise unable to find grit themselves, you will have to supply them with supplemental grit.

Grit is available at many of the same places that sell duck feed. Do not place the grit directly on the duck's food. Instead, provide the grit in a separate bowl and allow them to swallow the grit as necessary.

Oyster Shell

Crushed oyster shell is a calcium-rich supplement that some duck keepers like to provide their ducks. However, care should be taken to ensure that non-laying females and drakes are unable to eat significant amounts of oyster shell.

Oyster shell is provided to offset the calcium demands that the females experience during egg laying. Females that do not have sufficient dietary calcium will produce thin-shelled or pitted eggs. Weak eggs are less likely to hatch than those that are properly calcified. In extreme cases, calcium deficiencies can lead to egg binding.

Do not place the oyster shell powder on top of the ducks' food. Instead, place it in a small container and allow the ducks to eat it as they wish.

Instead of crushed oyster shell, some keepers place broken cuttlebone pieces in a dish for their ducks. Cuttlebone is another good source of calcium, but you must ensure that it is broken into small enough pieces.

Excess calcium can cause nearly as many problems as a deficiency can. Kidney disease often follows excess calcium intake. Accordingly, the best way to proceed is to provide your ducks with a healthy, varied diet that includes plenty of foraged greens. Many grasses and other wild-growing plants have a considerable amount of calcium.

If you are in doubt about the proper amount of calcium to provide your ducks, consult your veterinarian. Because calcium-related problems are hard to treat, an ounce of prevention, in this case, is really worth a pound of cure.

4. The Importance of Freshness

It is of paramount importance that only fresh, non-spoiled food is provided to your ducks. Molds and fungi can develop on commercial foods as well as raw fruits and vegetables.

Always be careful to purchase food from a reliable retailer and keep the bag sealed tightly between uses. Do not purchase duck food from questionable sources, and always be wary of foods that have drastically reduced prices.. Often, retailers mark down the price of commercial animal foods as they approach their expiration date.

Do not purchase very large bags if you only have a few ducks; the small savings will not be helpful if you cannot feed the food before it expires. Try to keep and store the food in the bag it is packaged in, but if you must transfer it, always mark the container with the food's expiration date. Discard any unused food afterwards (Hilary S. Stern, 2014).

Use common sense when storing fresh fruits, vegetables or "people food." Do not offer your ducks anything that you would not feel comfortable eating yourself. Anything that is slimy, molded, discolored or foul smelling should be discarded.

Fresh fruits and vegetables can be placed in sealed containers and then frozen for future use. Freezing will greatly extend the length of time that the food will stay suitable, but it may compromise the nutritional value slightly.

Chapter 8: Interacting with Your Pet Duck

Ducks have a reputation for being slightly pugnacious, in comparison to some of their Duck-derived relatives. While some Ducks can be defensive, proud animals that use their size to their advantage, many properly raised Ducks become loving companions.

Ducks do not like being picked up, and they will take great lengths to discourage you from trying to do so. Ducks are large birds – especially males – and they can inflict injuries with their sharp toenails. Additionally, their flapping wings and pecking beaks can affect an impressive defense.

To add insult to potential injury, most Ducks will expel the contents of their cloaca upon being lifted. This semi-liquid mixture is a powerful example of natural chemical warfare, the smell of which would probably be effective in dispersing angry mobs. Even those who have spent their lives working with animals and their accompanying waste often find duck droppings to be particularly foul smelling.

This means that holding Ducks is not something to do regularly (small ducklings are a different matter that will be covered below). Ducks are not rabbits, lap dogs or cats, and they do not feel any urge to snuggle with you – it is important that parents and children understand this at the outset.

Accordingly, it is important to understand the best way to move your ducks and pick them up when necessary. Learning the proper techniques ensures that you and your feathered companions get through such encounters with as little stress as possible.

1. Handling Young Ducklings

During the process of raising young ducks, it will often be necessary to move them from one place to another. Fortunately, for the first few months of their lives, Ducks can be held without great difficulty. They may still defecate when lifted off the ground, but because they are small, it is easier to keep the "yucky end" pointed away from you.

Ornery young ducks may peck at the hand that holds them, but they usually learn that you mean them no harm and stop the behavior with time. While the pecking may be off-putting to youngsters, it is a relatively harmless defense mechanism.

To lift a young duck, grip it firmly but gently by the sides, to keep the young bird from flapping its wings. Very small ducks can be grasped by one hand, while older ducklings may require the use of two hands. Allow the feet to slide between your fingers, or gently fold the legs into your hand.

2. Herding Your Ducks

Once they are mature, the best approach to keeping Ducks is to avoid picking them up or otherwise handling them, unless absolutely necessary.

As with moving any animals, the easiest way to do so is to convince them to move themselves. This is not hard with ducks; they are seemingly always on the move. The problem arises when you need to get them to move where you want them to move. Essentially, you must learn to be a "duck herder."

While they will never be accused of being as smart as dogs, dolphins or chimpanzees, Ducks are surprisingly intelligent, and quick to learn routines. In fact, establishing routines is one of the best ways to make herding an easy task.

Ideally, when you open the bird's safe, secure sleeping quarters early in the morning, the ducks will walk outside and move in a more-or-less straight line to their daytime activity area. They should willingly march through the door and be on their way to eating, drinking, swimming and generally being a duck. You can then – ideally – shut the gate behind them without ever having to put your hands on a duck.

In the late afternoon, they should already be anticipating your arrival at the gate or door, and be ready to make the trek back to their sleeping quarters. Upon reaching the roost, a perfect flock makes its way inside and settles down for the night with very little encouragement necessary.

Ducks largely "go with the flow" so it is very helpful to herd flocks of some size. The ducks will take social cues from their neighbors, reinforcing their tendency to walk where you want them to go.

Begin teaching the ducks these behaviors from a very young age. If you begin training your ducks to move from place to place at a young age, they will be much easier to herd when they are larger. Additionally, by virtue of their small size, the young ducklings are easier to control when this begins.

The easiest way to get your ducks accustomed to moving from one place to the other is to bribe them. For example, the ducks will usually be eager to exit their night roost once morning arrives. However, you will have to encourage them to go where you want them to go.

So, when you open the roost in the morning, move swiftly to the area you want the ducks to come to and lure them to follow with some of their favorite food. After doing this for a few days, they will begin to anticipate the routine and will naturally head to that area. Eventually, you can stop feeding them, once the behavior is the normal routine.

Stragglers who wander off or do not seem to be interested in the tasty treat require different strategies. Usually, ducks will flee when approached, so you can use this to your advantage.

While you are 20 yards (18 meters) or more away, begin circling behind the wandering Duck, so that the duck is between you and where you want it to go. For example, if the duck were at the center of a watch dial and you want it to go towards the 12 o'clock position, move so that you are standing at the 6 o'clock position.

Slowly start moving towards the duck. Usually, the Duck will begin to walk away from you, and towards the intended location. If other ducks are still heading in the same direction, it will help accelerate the process. The goal is not to stress, harass or frighten the bird. Rather, through gentle persuasion, get the 'Scovy to do as you wish.

If the duck begins veering off course, adjust your position to keep it between you and the target area. Sometimes it can help to have a long stick or pole when doing so. With the long stick, tap the ground to get the duck back on track.

For example, if the duck begins moving off to the left, put the pole in your left hand. Using the increased reach offered by the stick, extend the tip of the stick past the duck on the left, in order to encourage him to bring his course back to the right. Do not touch the bird with the stick, instead the goal is for the bird to see the stick and move the other way.

Some Duck keepers employ dogs to herd their birds. This is a wonderful option if you have a dog who is suitable and trustworthy enough for the job. In addition to helping to herd the ducks, the dog will likely dissuade predators to some extent. Well-trained dogs that have bonded with the flock can provide effective security for the ducks.

3. Lifting, Holding, Transporting and Catching Your Duck

Even the tamest Ducks are averse to being lifted from the ground or held. Unfortunately, there are times when you will have to coral, capture and hold your Ducks to inspect their health or move them.

Try to avoid stressing your birds unnecessarily when catching them. One of the best times to do so is during the night, when they will be slightly disoriented. If it is not possible to do so at night, consider herding the ducks into a room or building in which the lights can be turned off. Leave the lights off for about one hour before entering and trying to lift the animal.

If you are unable to catch your duck (many Ducks are surprisingly agile and able to sneak away from you no matter how close you get) use the corralling technique to get the job done.

Corralling your duck relies on gently herding it into an area where the walls function as a funnel. You can construct such a funnel with boards or any other barrier.

Once the ducks enter the wide end of the funnel, gently encourage them to travel to the narrow end. By doing so, the bird will become trapped, allowing you to get your hands on them.

4. Lifting Your Duck

Unlike chickens, who are often lifted by the legs, the legs of ducks are not strong enough to withstand this treatment. Lifting a duck by the legs may result in broken legs or feet.

Instead, to lift your duck, grip it by the body. Approach the bird calmly to avoid startling it or encouraging it to flee. Grab the bird gently by the sides, keeping the wings folded flat against the birds' sides. Once you have the duck lifted off the ground, place one of your hands under the bird and gently grasp the feet. This will reduce the chances of being scratched by the duck's long toe nails.

Some prefer to let the duck's feet protrude through the fingers, while others prefer to cup the feet in their hands, folding them up against the duck's body. Either technique will work.

Once the duck's feet are secure, press the duck lightly against your body, allowing your arm to keep one wing pressed flat, while your body contains the other wing. This one-handed style allows your free hand to open and close doors, inspect injuries or any number of other tasks.

When releasing your duck, place it down gently. Dropping your duck roughly can cause them significant injury.

5. Transporting Your Pet

From time to time, you may find it necessary to move your duck. For example, you may be forced to take your duck to the veterinarian; or, if you own a particularly beautiful specimen, a competitive show. Either case requires that you have appropriate travel accommodations for your pet. There are two basic choices of duck-transportation-containers: plastic tubs and wire cages.

Plastic Tubs

Plastic transportation tubs are easy to make, and can often be created from recycled or repurposed materials, making them quite affordable. To transform a tub into a duck-carrier, simply drill several 1-inch holes on the top and sides of the tub to provide ventilation. By placing the holes in this manner, air will be drawn in through the sides and vented out through the holes in the lid.

Place some dry straw at the bottom of the tub to provide comfort and to absorb liquids.

If not properly ventilated, this type of transportation vessel can become very damp and full of polluted air that can make your duck very sick.

Opaque tubs are the best choice, as they will prevent the ducks from seeing the activity outside the container. This can stress them, making them more susceptible to illness. Transparent containers can be used, but they should be covered with a lightweight covering to prevent the ducks from becoming stressed.

Wire Cages

Wire cages are perhaps the most popular choice for transporting ducks. These are available commercially in a variety of styles, sizes and price points. The other primary benefits of wire cages are that they offer plenty of ventilation for the inhabitants, which can make them more comfortable in warm environments. However, the open nature of the cage means that these are messier than plastic tubs and odors, spilled water, food and feces are likely to escape the boundaries of the cage from time to time. In cold weather, such cages cannot be left exposed to the elements for extended periods of time.

Transportation Safety

Regardless of the type of transportation vessel you use, always be sure that the container is securely strapped into your vehicle, by using seatbelts, bungee cords or straps. In addition to keeping your ducks safer in the event of an accident, it will help prevent the container from sliding around – something that can cause you to have an accident in the first place!

Never leave ducks unattended in a hot car. The glass windows create a greenhouse effect, which can cause the internal temperature to rise to dangerous levels very quickly. Ducks can and have died from being left in a hot car.

Avoid playing loud music or driving erratically while chauffeuring your ducks. Ultimately, a car ride can be a very stressful experience for your feathered friends, and you should try to keep the event as stress-free as possible.

Aggressive Males

Sometimes, male Ducks become very aggressive during the breeding season. Fueled by hormones and an instinct to challenge all rivals, drakes occasionally display antagonist behaviors towards their keepers. Drakes of this mindset may run at or even chase people, flap their wings and peck at the "offending" humans.

While usually a small inconvenience that will disappear as the season progresses, these actions can frighten some people. Additionally, the ducks could cause minor injuries, particularly if their feet and long toenails are involved in the altercation.

There are two basic strategies for dealing with this problem. The first is to simply provide the duck with some extra space until his hormones calm down. However, this is not always possible. In such cases, it may be more effective to restrain the bird.

The reason the drake is attacking you is that he sees you as a competing male. A problem that arises from partially imprinting on humans, the best way to correct the behavior is to convince him that you are the dominant male (even if you are a woman), not him.

Do this by refusing to back away from the duck when he charges. You may push him back or even grab his body and hold him to the ground for a few minutes.

Take care that you do not hurt your drake, or stress him unnecessarily. Think of it as a wrestling match, where the goal is to simply get him to give up and look for someone else to pick on (which will often be one of the females).

6. Feather Clipping and Pinioning

Besides providing a completely enclosed habitat, there are only two ways to keep your Ducks from flying away: pinioning their wings or clipping their flight feathers.

Pinioning refers to the removal of the distal segment of the birds' wings. The process renders the birds flightless, and need only be performed once, but it is a very traumatic experience for the duck.

This practice is unpalatable to many duck owners, who find it cruel. Additionally, the practice may be illegal in some areas. If you do decide to pinion your ducks, be sure that a properly qualified veterinarian performs the procedure.

It is best to pinion birds when they are very young, if possible. However, the activity can cause so much stress that some youngsters die shortly after the procedure. Often, breeders will pinion the wings of your ducks before you purchase them for a small fee.

By contrast, clipping a duck's flight feathers is harmless and just as effective at keeping the ducks from flying away. The only down side of clipping feathers, as opposed to pinioning, is that it must be performed every year. An additional benefit of clipping the birds' feathers is that you can perform this procedure yourself.

Have someone knowledgeable about birds demonstrate feather clipping the first time. In principle, the primary flight feathers are cut off with a pair of sharp scissors. Usually, the feathers on one wing are clipped, while the feathers on the other wing are left intact.

By removing just a few feathers, these large and heavy ducks become unable to achieve the necessary lift to fly.

If you do not wish to clip the bird's feathers yourself, most veterinarians and pet stores will provide the service for a small fee.

Some keepers elect to accept the possibility that their birds may fly away, as they do not appreciate the alternative. Another reason that some keepers opt for not pinioning or clipping their duck's wings is that they do not want to "disarm" the birds. This is particularly common among keepers who allow their ducks to live in a free-range manner.

The idea is that if a fox, coyote or other land based predator threatens the ducks, they have a better chance of escaping if they have the ability to fly. Even though large drakes cannot get very far from the ground, intact wings will allow them to move and maneuver much more effectively than those who have had their wings altered.

7. Handling and Hygiene

Like most other animals, ducks can carry germs that can make people sick. Some of these germs do not even make the ducks sick, but they can be very dangerous for people. It is always important to practice good hygiene to reduce the chances of contracting an illness.

Many ducks (and other birds) carry Salmonella bacteria in their digestive system. The bacteria is spread via the fecal-oral route, meaning that ducks pass the bacteria in their feces, where it can eventually make its way into the mouth of another duck.

As the ducks excrete infective spores in their droppings, they find their way onto the duck's feathers, feet and beaks, as well as throughout their habitats. The entire area should be considered to be covered in the bacteria.

If some of the bacteria gets on your skin, and then you inadvertently transfer some of it to your mouth, you can get sick. It only takes a few spores to cause the illness, so it can be quite easy to catch.

Accordingly, you must be sure to wash your hands after handling poultry or anything in their enclosure. Use an anti-bacterial soap and warm water. Be sure to scrub the tiny nooks and crannies of your hands, where bacteria are likely to persist. This includes your fingernails and the crevices in your knuckles.

It is a good idea to wash your clothing after interacting with the ducks as well. Some keepers keep a pair of slip-on boots handy for when they must enter the enclosure. This way, they do not have to wash their shoes repeatedly.

Salmonella is usually not very serious for healthy adults. However, young children, the elderly and those with compromised immune systems are extremely susceptible to the disease, and often develop serious complications. In rare cases, death can result.

The most common symptoms of the disease are gastrointestinal upset, abdominal cramps and a high fever. Most healthy adults recover from the disease without medical attention, but antibiotics and supportive care may be necessary for high-risk groups.

With this in mind, the Center for Disease Control and Prevention recommends that all live poultry be kept outdoors, and away from areas where people eat or drink. Furthermore, the CDC advises that children under 5 years of age be prevented from touching live poultry.

According to the CDC, live poultry are one of the most likely ways for people to contract the disease. Since the 1990s, more than 45 different outbreaks of the bacteria have originated from live poultry. These outbreaks have caused more than 220 hospitalizations and five deaths (Centers for Disease Control and Prevention, 2014).

Never, under any circumstances, should you use kitchen or bathroom sinks to wash tools or other accessories that have been in contact with the ducks.

Sometimes, a new bird may have infections that will prove fatal to ducks and other fowl present in your farm or garden. The only way to overcome this is by taking adequate measures to quarantine.

Quarantining requires you to keep the new bird away from the rest of the birds for at least 2 to 3 weeks. During this period, your new bird will require a separate coop or house to ensure that he does not mingle with the birds. Many duck owners neglect quarantining to avoid the expense of an additional coop. However, it is worth the investment considering that the entire existing flock is in danger of infection.

8. Understanding Imprinting

The concept of imprinting is rather interesting. The process of this phenomenon is yet to be explained. Nobody knows what exactly happens in the brain of the duck when an imprint is formed. The first and the strongest type of imprint is the filial imprint.

Filial Imprinting is a certain belief pattern in these ducks. As soon as these birds hatch, the first being that they see is recognized as their mother. If you remember watching baby ducks in the wild or even in films, they follow their mothers around and are very keen on obtaining the attention of their mother. Now, it is not necessary that the mother has to be a duck. If you are the first being that a duck sees upon hatching, it is automatically imprinted in its brain that you are mom. Of course, these ducklings are unable to recognize the face or voice of their imprinted parent. However, they will follow you around and expect you to be their mom.

Now, some of you may think that imprinting might be true in case of dogs and cats or other pets, too. After all, they are equally attached to their owners. However, there is one very distinct difference between other animals and birds like ducks and geese.

No matter how attached a dog or cat is to you, it will always recognize itself as a dog or cat respectively. However, when a duckling forms an imprint, it believes that it is the same creature

106

as its parent. So if the imprint formed is that of a human, a duck will believe that he is human.

Even if there are other ducks present around it, the ducking never sees them as parents. It is possible for the duck to understand that he is not a human but is a duck, when he is around others of his own species. However, the filial imprint is only of the being he saw first. The other ducks are only imprinted as his siblings. He will learn and play with his siblings. However, the beauty of this breed is that he will love his 'mom' the most.

If you are planning to hatch eggs, remember that your responsibility does not end with successfully bringing a duckling into this world. Remember that if the baby sees you first after hatching, you are in for a long term commitment. You will have to play the role of the duckling's mother. Therefore, if you are planning on incubating and hatching a duck egg to bring home a duckling, there are a few things that you must ask yourself.

Do You Have the Time?

Once the duckling believes that you are mom, you are in this relationship for the long run. This is actually a full time job. You will have to sleep next to the duckling, play with him outdoors, eat with him, ensure that he is warm, console him when he is crying and even learn to speak the language of the ducking. The only possible break you will get is a short time away from the duckling when he is in the hands of a trained and experienced duck sitter.

Do You Have the Patience?

There is no way you can litter box train your pet. They are also not capable of controlling their poop. They will mess up your home. Despite being the parent, you cannot even think of disciplining these babies. Even a gentle flick or smack can injure their delicate bills and bones. You might be tempted to use duck diapers but be assured that your babies will absolutely resent it.

Do You Have the Resources?

Although your duckling thinks he is a human, the truth is that he will grow up to be a fully grown duck whose needs are just the same as any other duck. You must be able to give him a shelter that is free from predators. It is your job to ensure that he eats well and gets the required healthcare. There are also several additional expenses that you will be responsible for.

If you wish to parent a duckling, you must be completely committed. It is also your responsibility to ensure that your duckling interacts with his own species for breeding purposes in the future. You must have the permission of your neighbors and your landlord to have ducks in your home. Remember that they can be quite noisy. If you have pets at home, you are responsible for the safety of the duckling and your pet.

The concept of filial imprinting is quite adorable. However, the responsibility of the parent is far more than taking care of the bird. There is another important concept known as sexual imprinting that you must also be aware of to ensure that your duck grows up and picks the right mate for himself. Although this seems quite natural in the animal world, the way a duck thinks will bewilder you.

Sexual Imprinting

Sexual imprinting is a very important phenomenon in reproduction and breeding. It is through sexual imprinting that a certain species recognizes the attractive features in an opposite gender of the same species. It is with this understanding of attractive features that the bird picks the right mate when it is mature.

With ducks, sexual imprinting works quite differently. The roots of sexual imprinting lie in filial imprinting. Now, if the duck recognizes another duck as its mom, there lies no issue. However, in case the filial imprint is that of a human, it is a task for the human to help this duckling grow up to recognize his own species as desirable to mate with.

If you are planning to hatch an egg, you must make sure that there are several other ducks that this duckling can grow around. In case this does not happen, the duckling will view the features of the human as attractive. So, there are high chances that he will court other people or even the parent instead of other ducks. He might find his entire species altogether unattractive. Therefore, you must be very knowledgeable about the phenomenon of imprinting.

Chapter 9: Breeding Ducks

Breeding your Ducks can be a fun and educational way to enjoy your pets, increase the size of your flock, supplement your dinner table with fresh duck eggs or make a little extra money by selling the chicks that result. In fact, given a healthy, mature flock and proper husbandry, your female ducks will deposit eggs, whether you want them to or not.

There Is Not Much to It

Unlike some other exotic pets, Ducks do not require any special pre-breeding conditioning to reproduce successfully. As spring approaches and the length of the daylight increases each day, the females' bodies begin preparing to deposit eggs. If you have a drake present, he will breed the females, producing fertile eggs. However, even if no drake is present, or a drake is present but does not successfully breed the females, the females must deposit their eggs.

The breeding instincts of ducks are strong. If kept in enclosures without suitable mates, ducks often engage in same-sex dominance behaviors that superficially resemble mating activity.

Social Concerns

One of the duck keeper's primary jobs during the breeding season is ensuring that the drake does not wound or stress the females. Drakes can be very aggressive in their breeding advances, so you must watch the females for signs of stress or injury. If you notice some of the females are losing feathers, exhibit wounds on their neck, lose significant weight or show signs of stress (loss of appetite, withdrawal, etc.) separate the male to allow them to recover.

If you house more than one male in the same enclosed space, you must ensure that conflicts between them remain "civilized." While posturing, crest raising and chasing are unlikely to cause significant injury, it is possible for males to injure each other. This is especially important if the drakes are not of the same size or social status. A smaller, weaker male must be able to retreat from the dominant drake.

Normally, males work out their differences without many problems. Subordinate males often form bachelor groups that spend most of their time at the periphery of the flock. However, every situation and animal is different, so it pays to be diligent. Often, visual barriers and ample room are sufficient to diffuse tensions and promote flock harmony. Additionally, it is helpful to ensure that there are at least two females for every drake.

Nesting

As egg deposition time approaches, female Ducks will begin looking for a suitable nesting location. It is best to provide a proper location that is easy to locate, easy to access and safe for the ducks. Otherwise, the female may deposit the eggs somewhere inappropriate, dangerous or impossible to find.

Wild Duck females use hollow cavities in trees and logs as egg deposition sites. Keep this in mind when preparing your ducks' nesting boxes.

There are many different ways to construct egg-laying boxes (these boxes are also called brooding boxes, because the female will use the boxes to keep the young warm after they hatch). Some keepers build elaborate wooden boxes, while others repurpose plastic dog houses or barrels. In all cases, the boxes must address the same set of concerns:

• The ducks want somewhere dark, secure and appropriately sized. The larger the box is, the more secure it must feel to the ducks. Accomplish this by blocking as many sight lines as possible.

• The nest box must remain as dry as possible while in use. The mother may track some water into the box, but it should dry as soon as possible. Be sure that the box has some airflow to prevent stagnant conditions and accelerate the drying process.

• It is advantageous to use some sort of small barrier at the entrance to the box, for example, a 2x4 piece of lumber, placed on the ground across the entranceway. This will help keep the nest box clean and help contain the hatchlings as they begin moving about. The barrier should be easy for the mother to cross.

• The egg-laying box can be placed directly on bare ground, grass, concrete or wood shavings. Alternatively, you can use an egg box that contains a connected floor. Place some straw or grass clippings on the ground so that the female can form them into a nest.

• Many keepers find that it is helpful to provide more egg-laying boxes than ducks. This helps to keep the ducks from fighting over locations or choosing to lay their eggs outside of a nest box.

• Place the nest boxes in quiet areas that are easy to access. By placing the nest boxes near large structures, such as buildings or large trees, they will benefit from additional protection from the elements. Additionally, the shade will keep the nesting box more secure.

• It is essentially impossible to protect a nesting box from predators if the birds are housed in a free-range style. Accordingly, some keepers elect to move nesting females to secure pens during the laying season.

- Once the female has found a suitable nesting location, she will form the substrate to her liking and pad the bottom with a carpet of down.

Sex Change in Ducks

It has been observed quite often by duck owners that their female duck undergoes a gender change. Several animal behavior specialists relate this drastic change to a rather drastic reaction to the forceful and aggressive sex that drakes engage in.

You will observe the occurrence of a tail curl in the ducks and also the appearance of drake coloring. Most often, when sex change occurs, the ducks will also stop laying eggs. This is one of those unsolved mysteries of nature. However, several scientists and waterfowl experts have linked this change to hormonal imbalance.

One theory is that the hens usually have two ovaries. Only one of them is active while the other one is benign. The benign ovary begins to produce testosterone, causing the appearance of male like features in the female ducks. Of course, the primary sexual organs are never developed. This transformed female is able to sire offspring's either. It is only a development of secondary sexual characteristics that occurs.

Questions to Ask Yourself

Undoubtedly, raising and breeding ducks is a popular occupation across the globe. There are several individuals who will swear by the large benefits that they reaped by simply rearing ducks and trading their eggs. If you are also considering breeding ducks, you can prepare yourself for a rather lucrative business. However, before you actually start breeding ducks, there are some questions that you may want to ask yourself:

- How will I reap profits from the ducks that I am raising?
- What is the breeding purpose?
- Are there enough funds to take care of the birds?

113

- Do I need additional manpower to run my breeding business? If yes, can I afford the costs of hiring people?
- How safe will the ducks be from predators?
- Do I need any licenses to breed ducks?
- What certification does my breeding program require?
- Will my neighbors be disturbed?

When you have found the answers to these questions, you will be able to decide if breeding ducks is a good idea for you or not. Rearing ducks is very different from having other pets and you must be entirely equipped to provide your ducks with the right care.

The Advantages of Breeding

Breeding Ducks has picked up as a popular vocation across the globe because of the obvious benefits that are associated with it. Ducks are also preferred over other poultry or several reasons. The advantages of choosing duck breeding are:

- **Ducks are easy to handle:** Unlike other poultry, ducks are less demanding. If you have a flock of ducks, you will notice that they are rather content in the company of one another. Other poultry, however, is attention seeking. They are also extremely sensitive because of which they need extra care.

- **Ducks are not high maintenance:** Other farm fowl and poultry are not as rough and tough as ducks. Usually ducks are immune to avian diseases that easily infect other poultry. While ducks do require a great deal of healthcare, they are not as expensive to maintain as other poultry.

- **Ducks are highly adaptable:** Ducks, especially, are known for their ability to survive in diverse environmental conditions. This makes it a lot easier for the owners who do not have to go out of the way to make the ducks feel comfortable and content.

- **Profits from Eggs:** Breeding ducks is also a lot more lucrative than breeding other poultry. Ducks lay a lot more eggs than poultry like chicken. On an average, a duck will lay around 8 to 10 eggs each day. This means that you will get at least 150 eggs in one single reproduction cycle.

- **Better behaved:** In comparison to other poultry, ducks are much better behaved. They are pleasant to have around the farm. The only time ducks display aggressive behavior is when they are in the middle of a reproduction cycle.

- **Hatchlings are easier to raise:** Taking care of the hatchlings is much easier with ducks as they are more adaptable. So, if you are new to breeding ducks are the more suited option.

Duck breeding is considered ideal if you are new to the whole concept of breeding. Since the demands are lesser with ducks, they make for a great practice run before you move on to other poultry.

Types of Breeding

There are two breeding options that you will come across: Natural Breeding and Selective Breeding.

Depending upon the purpose of your breeding program you may choose between the two types. In case of natural breeding, the In case of natural breeding, the ducks mate with only their own kind. Over several decades, there are modifications in the traits and the features of the offspring depending upon the survival needs. As per Charles Darwin, only the birds with the most suitable features for survival would sustain.
In case of artificial breeding, the breeders will induce desirable

characteristics from other species to create hybrids. You may indulge in this type of breeding if your primary purpose is to create ducks for exhibition. When you choose artificial breeding, make sure that you are equipped with all the necessary information. If the breeding is not carried out properly, the mutation could be so severe that the resulting offspring may not even be strong enough to survive.

Chapter 10: Ducks Eggs

If you are planning to bring home Ducks in order to gain a profit with the eggs that are laid, you must be well informed about the care required to maintain and collect these eggs. Some of you may also be interested in raising a flock of Ducks in your backyard. In that case, you must know how to hatch the eggs and take proper care of the hatchlings that are produced. Let us take a close look at all the important facts associated with Duck eggs.

Nutritional Value:

- Protein per egg: 9.5 gms
- 108-130 calories
- Cholesterol : 619 mg
- Fat: 7.3 gms
- Vitamins B6, B12, A, D, E
- 8 essential amino acids
- Phosphorous and Calcium
- Sulphur
- Zinc
- Potassium
- Iron

Collecting the Eggs

During the breeding season, each hen will lay about 8 to 10 eggs per day. This means that you will get an average of 150 eggs every year. One thing you need to remember about ducks is that the laying of the egg is not restricted to the nest. For those who are interested in an egg business, this is a matter of utmost concern as the eggs must be collected immediately after they are laid. If you fail to do this, chances are that the eggs will be damaged before you collect them.

Usually, ducks will lay eggs either late in the night or in the wee hours of the morning. If the duck is still laying eggs, you might want to wait for at least two hours so that the eggs have enough time to roost. When you collect the eggs, make sure you do so in a plastic egg tray. Separate the dirty eggs from the clean ones to make your job easier.

If the eggs you are selecting are particularly meant for incubation, you must also check the weight of the egg. If it is even cracked or molted, you must choose another egg for incubation. Eggs with even the slightest deformities are less likely to develop into hatchlings.

Once the eggs have been collected, the next thing to do is clean them. Remember that there are several microbes on the surface of the egg. If the egg is not sufficiently cleaned, there are chances that they will creep in through the shell to spoil the egg. Make sure you get rid of all the mud and manure using steel wool. You may even wipe the eggs.

Remember, washing the eggs is not an option as the contents can be damaged. Choose fumigation if you think that the egg needs thorough cleaning.

Storage

The next thing to worry about is storage. If you want to incubate the eggs, you need to have a decent number. You must wait until you have a few eggs before you begin the incubation process. It is possible to store the eggs for a maximum of seven days provided that humidity and temperature is controlled. The ideal storage temperature for duck eggs is 13 degrees Celsius when the humidity is maintained at 75%.

Dealing with the Eggs

Soon after the female begins sitting on the nest, she will start to deposit one egg each day. Your next step will depend on your goals.

The simplest course of action is to let nature simply take its course. Leave the mother alone and allow her to brood her eggs and hatchlings as she sees fit. Some mothers will prove to be better mothers than others are, and you may lose eggs or hatchlings along the way.

If you would like to harvest the eggs for eating, you can simply remove the new egg each day. The female may continue depositing eggs for some time this way.

Alternatively, you can remove the eggs once she is done with the laying process. The eggs do not begin developing until the last egg has been deposited.

Other keepers prefer to remove the eggs and incubate them inside. Duck eggs are somewhat difficult to incubate, but it is possible.

If you do not want to breed the ducks, and you do not care for their delicious eggs, you will need to render them unviable. To do so, wait until the female leaves the nest each day to eat, drink and bathe. While she is gone, shake each egg vigorously, and return it to the nest.

Shaking the egg will rupture the blood vessels inside, preventing the egg from developing into a chick. It is important to return the eggs to the nest after shaking them, or the female will just move to another location and deposit another clutch of eggs.

Duck eggs are rather large, as would be expected from such large ducks. Ducks produce eggs that contain about three percent more yolk and one percent more shell mass than those of Ducks.

Some keepers like to place protective structures around brooding females to prevent predators from attacking her or the eggs. While the female will often leave the nest when confronted by a large predator (who will then eat most or all of the eggs) they occasionally stick around and try to defend their nest. When this happens, the females often sustain serious injuries, and may not even succeed in protecting the eggs.

Snakes, weasels, raccoons and dogs are frequent predators of duck eggs. Most will attack the nest at night, so you may consider allowing the mother to have her freedom during the day so that she can get food and water and stretch her legs a bit. Then, shortly before nightfall, you can place some sort of "tent" over the female to provide some protection.

If you find that predators are a frequent problem, you may need to enclose the entire area that holds the breeding females. The only other reasonable course of action is to employ the talents of a well-trained guard dog.

Hatching the Eggs

Usually Ducks will start laying eggs when they are about 7 months old. They are prolific egg layers and will lay about 150-200 hundred eggs each year. Collecting these eggs and hatching them successfully is a challenge. There are two options for hatching the eggs:

- Natural Incubation
- Artificial incubation

Natural Incubation

Brooding is the process when a female actually sits on the eggs to hatch them. There are some obvious signs that you can look out for when your hen is ready to brood. To begin with, she will stop laying eggs. She will also make a very distinct quacking noise. She also sits on the eggs without budging. There must not be more than 15 eggs on each nest in order to increase hatchability of the eggs. Once the hen begins to brood, she will provide the eggs with the necessary moisture and heat for the eggs to hatch.

There are some things that you must take care of when you have a broody hen:

- The hen should be kept close to food and water
- The nutritional requirements of the brooding ducks must be taken care of.
- Regularly check the ducks for parasites and also for infections

After the first week of brooding, you must check if the eggs are fertile. All you have to do is hold them up against any bright light. If you are able to see a dark shape in the egg, you can be certain that it is fertile. If the egg is clear, it is infertile.

Artificial Incubation

Ducks will not become broody if the eggs are collected regularly. In such cases, you must opt for artificial incubation. You can make use of commercial incubators to hatch the eggs. These incubators vary in capacity and most often depend upon fuels like gas or kerosene and even electricity to provide heat. The temperature of the device may be controlled with the help of a thermostat that comes with the incubator. The Duck egg will take about 28 days to hatch when kept in an incubator.

When you remove the eggs are from storage, ensure that they are kept in room temperature for at least 6 hours before they are transferred in to the incubator. The temperature must be set to 37.5 degree Celsius and must be reduced by 0.2 degrees in case of hatchers.

Humidity must also be maintained perfectly. If it is excessive, the eggs won't be dry enough to hatch. If humidity is less, the eggs will dry too quickly. There are special moisture trays to control humidity. Ideally it should be set at 70% relative humidity.

The eggs in the incubator must be turned everyday to make sure that the contents do not adhere to the shell. Generally, it is recommended that the eggs are turned at an angle of 90 degrees. This process can be made automatic with the help of turning equipment that will turn the eggs every hour.

Make sure you constantly check the egg fertilization by shining a light on them. Fumigation is an important process in artificial incubation. Use a mixture of formalin and potassium permanganate to make sure that harmful bacteria, especially salmonella is completely removed.

Removing the hatch from the Incubator

Prepare a brooder with the required heat source when the eggs are close to the hatching date. The average hatchability in ducks is usually about 70%. The hatch must be transferred to the brooder almost as soon as it the process is complete.

Even if the eggs are hatched by natural incubation, brooders are necessary. When the eggs approach the hatching date, you will see that the hen sits on them for shorter periods of time. The hen will spend maximum time away from the nest.

When the ducklings have hatched, special grower's pellets should be given as feed to meet the nutritional requirements. These pellets contain the necessary nutrients and minerals that ensure proper development in the ducklings. When the ducklings are about five weeks old, you can introduce wheat with grit. Grit usually consists of oyster shells and help provide the roughage necessary to break the food down while digesting.

Should you avoid artificial incubation?

Several breeders prefer natural incubation even though there are no recorded issues with artificial insemination. Sometimes Ducks may stop brooding. In such cases, you can reintroduce them to nesting and brooding using model eggs and even rocks. Eggs can be incubated naturally using certain breeds of chicken as well. Make sure you check the brooding and mothering history of the chicken that you choose as the brooder.

Will my Duck Stop Laying Eggs?

For those whose primary interest lies in earning through the eggs that are available in the breeding season, this is a matter of great concern. Although Ducks have been known for their amazing egg laying abilities, there are some occasions when they simply will not produce any eggs. If this occurs, the first thing to do would be taking you Duck to a waterfowl expert. Most often, reproductive disorders and other health disorders will result in your Duck not laying any eggs. However, there are several other factors that might have lead to a stop in egg laying:

• **The Age of the Bird**: the number of eggs laid will reduce as the duck ages and may eventually come to a halt.

• **Parasites**: If your duck is suffering from any problem related to parasites and ticks, she might be unable to produce healthy eggs. In some cases, the entire process of egg formation is hindered, leading to a stop in the laying of eggs.

• **Weather Conditions**: Ducks are able to produce eggs only when they have ample warmth. In case the weather is not suitable for your duck to produce eggs you can expect her to be unable to do so.

• **Change in Diet:** If you are contemplating a change in your duck's diet, it must be done gradually. You must also make sure that the duck has enough time until the breeding season to get used to a certain kind of diet. If the nutrition is not adequate or is different from what your duck is used to, there is a hindrance in the production of the egg.

- **New Birds in the Flock:** When you introduce new ducks into the flock, it is a big change for the existing ducks. When ducks interact in a group, they tend to be extremely social and also form a pecking order with the other ducks. When you introduce one or more new ducks, this equation changes. The ducks get severely stressed at time and will stop laying eggs for some time until this pecking order has been re-established.

- **Change in Routine:** Ducks are highly disciplined creatures. They need to be fed at a certain time and must also be allowed to roost at a certain time. However, if you make any significant change in any part of their routine, it leads to severe stress, making them stop laying eggs.

- **Improper Husbandry**: If the pen is unclean or overcrowded, the number of eggs laid will reduce significantly. In addition to that, if the conditions of the pen are too dark or cold, it results in stress and illness. As a result, egg laying is reduced considerably and may even stop if poor conditions persist.

- **Too Much Handling**: If you need to transport your birds, you must do it very carefully. During the transfer, they should not be handled too much or handled roughly. Laying is hindered if the transfer is stressful. In addition to that, a change in location also requires the duck to get accustomed to the new conditions, because of which, laying is significantly reduced.

- **Predators or Pests**: Like we mentioned in earlier chapters, ducks are at the bottom of the food cycle. As a result, they are easily frightened. If your duck has been attached by a predator or even feels threatened by one, you can expect a decline in egg laying. Most often, even pests like rats and rodents will result in stress.

- **The Hen is Broody**: This is a phase that most new duck owners are unaware of. Sometimes, if your duck suddenly stops her prolific egg laying, it is because she is ready for brooding. She is ready to nest the eggs and hatch them. Brooding reduces significantly when collecting of eggs is frequent. Usually, brooding is a habit with younger ducks.

So you see, even if the egg laying comes to a halt, it does not mean that your duck is a poor investment. It only means that you may have to review your husbandry practices or get your duck a good health check up. There are some things that you can do to maximize egg production among your Ducks. Some steps are extremely simple and will help maintain the cycle of egg production and keep it consistent.

Can I Increase Egg Laying?

There are several steps you can take as the breeder and the owner of your flock to make sure that the egg production is consistent. These simple measures are also very important in ensuring that your eggs are healthy and of great quality.

• **Improve The Quality Of The Feed:** When you purchase the feed from pet stores or the supermarket, you will see that there are several options available. You must make sure that you make no compromises on costs and other factors and only choose recommended duck feed pellets. Make sure that the feed is fresh, has no insects and mold in it and is also compliant with the recommended nutrient levels.

• **Ensure That Your Duck Get The Right Type Of Feed:** The type of food that you choose for your duck must be appropriate for its age. For instance, if you have chicks, make sure you feed them grower pellets instead of regular pellets. Also, maintain the quantity of the feed. On an average, a duck that is ready to lay eggs must be put on a controlled diet. She should be given not more than .35 pounds per day. If your duck becomes overweight, then there are chances that she will develop issues with fertility and egg production. The feed must be removed at the end of every single day while ensuring that it is available to them for the rest of the day.

- **Provide Plenty of Water:** Ducks are waterfowl and definitely require an ample supply of fresh water every day. Ducks use this water not only for drinking but will also swim in it when they want to. If you are unable to ensure that the water is clean, you will see that egg production is hindered. As I mentioned in the earlier chapters, water is required for ducks to regulate their body temperature. This body temperature is pivotal in the process of laying eggs. If the water is muddy or messy, your ducks will become stressed and depressed to an extent.

- **Ensure Proper Lighting:** Day length is an important concept for ducks that are breeding. Usually, a duck becomes sexually mature only when the length of the day begins to increase. This is between the months of January and June. When the day length begins to reduce, egg production also comes to a halt. If you want your ducks to continue laying eggs despite the available day length, you must make up for the lack of natural light with artificial light. Your Duck must have at least 17 hours of sunlight every day. This, of course, is greater than the natural light available too. So, in order for your duck to get comfortable with this day length, make sure you add ½ hour of light each day before sunrise and after sunset each week till you reach 17 hours of light

- **Keep Them Calm:** Ducks require a routine. In fact, they are quite fond of the concept of routines. You must give them the same feed each day, provide them with the same type of bedding, the same space to roost in and also the same lighting conditions. If you want your ducks to produce eggs regularly, it is recommended that you even put on the same clothes each time you go out to collect the eggs. Any change in the routine makes the ducks stressed and will reduce their abilities to lay eggs.

- **Do Not Have Too Many Males In The Group:** Usually, the recommended ratio of females to males is 1:5. This ratio must be maintained very strictly if not reduced. However, if you add more males to the group, they will become violent. In many cases, the females get severely injured because of the sexual aggressiveness in male ducks. As a result, the egg laying abilities come down and might even stop in severe cases.

Duck breeding and caring is a matter of great care and responsibility. However, it is quite easy to adapt to if you are able to understand what is best for your ducks. You can also get a lot of assistance from waterfowl experts who will be able to provide you with healthcare and advise to breed healthy ducks.

If you are ever unsure of what to do with your ducks or if you are witnessing recurring health issues, you can check with your local waterfowl expert. He should be able to help you make the right choices for your duck.

The number of eggs that your Duck lays depends entirely upon the conditions that prevail in your home. You must make sure that the ducks are calm and healthy. If you are sure that the duck does not have anything to worry about during the breeding season, you can be rest assured that you will be able to make great profits due to the numbers of eggs that you will get.

No matter what you do make sure that you prioritize the health and safety of your duck. Keep the environment and other husbandry practices at their best. That way, you will be able to rear healthy ducks that will thrive in almost all conditions. All you need to do is set a foundation that is cordial for your ducks to live and reproduce in. After that, you can enjoy the benefits of having Ducks on your farm.

If you are bringing home Ducks for an egg business, you must be patient. It is not something that will flourish overnight. You must be prepared for a few losses initially. Once you learn about handling the eggs properly, you will be able to run your business smoothly.

Chapter 11: Health Concerns for Ducks

In general, Ducks are very hardy animals. They do not suffer from very many health problems, and are usually resistant to pathogenic viruses, bacteria and fungi.

The best way to keep your Ducks healthy is by providing pristine living conditions and perfect husbandry. This will allow the ducks' immune systems to battle pathogens that they are exposed to.

1. Guidelines to Help Prevent Disease

It is impossible to eliminate the potential for disease transmission. However, by following these three guidelines, you can greatly reduce the risks to your pets, and give them a better chance at living long, healthy lives:

- Minimize the stress on your ducks, so that their immune systems operate at peak efficiency.

- Do not let your ducks socialize. Keep your Ducks away from all other waterfowl.

- Immunize the ducks against as many diseases as possible.

By examining the ways in which different diseases can infect 'Ducks, the reasons for these three guidelines are clear.

In broad terms, some infectious agents are ubiquitous, and only cause problems when they overwhelm an animal's immune system. This is most likely to occur in stressed animals, that do not have access to proper housing, or are fed improper diets. Coccidiosis is one example of this type of pathogen. It infects

129

most ducks, but usually only causes symptoms when a particularly lethal strain is ingested, or when the birds ingest large quantities of the sporulated oocysts (the infectious particles for these parasitic protozoans) (Larry R. McDougald, 2012).

Accordingly, it is important to provide your duck with a clean habitat, feed it the most nutritious diet possible, and ensure that they are protected from inclement weather and temperature extremes, to avoid these types of pathogens, and the illnesses they cause.

Other infectious agents must pass from one host to another, and are not likely to infect ducks that do not come into contact with other ducks. For example, a duck housed singly for the entirety of his life, who does not share water or space with other ducks, is unlikely to develop viral enteritis. However, a duck only needs to sip infected water once to become infected, and ultimately die.

Your flock will undoubtedly exchange germs amongst themselves, so you must effectively quarantine your flock. Try to purchase ducks from the same breeder or retailer, and avoid adding other members to the flock at a later time.

Take care to prevent wild ducks from sharing a pond with your flock. Additionally, be careful when visiting other places with ducks; a frequent way diseases are spread is via dirt particles that cling to people's shoes or clothing. Ensure that visitors have not recently been around other ducks.

Therefore, as explained in the first two guidelines, you should provide your ducks with the very best care possible, to ensure that your ducks' immune system is working as well as it can and that they do not share water, space or the company of other ducks.

Immunization is the process of injecting a dead, weakened or sub-infectious quantity of a virus into a potential host before it gets sick. When this occurs, the ducks' immune systems learn to fight off this virus, while not being at risk of becoming sick. This way, when the ducks eventually encounter the live virus, their immune systems defeat it, keeping them from getting sick.

Some vaccines provide lifetime immunity, while others must be given repeatedly to remain effective. Vaccines exist for duck viral hepatitis, duck viral enteritis and Riemerella anatipestifer infections, and others are under development (Major Viral Diseases of Waterfowl and Their Control, 2011).

By following these three guidelines, you are likely to reduce the chances of illness in your flock significantly.

2. Common Infectious Diseases

Ducks are remarkably resilient animals that are susceptible to relatively few infections and diseases. However, a few are more common than others, meaning that the keeper should pay particular attention to these maladies.

Coccidiosis

Coccidiosis is a protozoal disease that causes ducks to exhibit digestive problems, instability and depression. However, the best clue to the presence of the disease is bubbling from the eyes.

While adults often carry Coccidiosis asmptomatically, it can cause young animals to grow slowly or die. Coccidiosis is treatable with sulfa drugs. However, continuous use of a given drug often leads to the evolution of resistant strains of the pathogen.

Fortunately, a vaccine has been developed to help the birds fight off the infection, and the vaccine is gaining in popularity. Unfortunately, it appears that Ducks are unusually susceptible to the pathogen, which lives in the dirt, mud and water of their natural habitats.

Avian Influenza

Ducks can contract avian influenza, and there is a possibility that they can transmit this illness to humans. Since 1997, the Centers for Disease Control and Prevention states that humans have contracted several different strains of the disease.

While wild birds seldom die from the disease, avian influenza is often fatal to captive birds, who often develop more virulent strains of the virus. Waterfowl seem to be especially susceptible to the disease.

A 2001 report documented that the disease caused nervousness and death in a backyard flock of Ducks and domestic geese (Anser anser domestica). Upon further examination, the ducks were found to have incurred damage to their nervous systems and pancreases (Mutinelli, 2001).

Riemerella anatipestifer

Riemerella anatipestifer is a bacterial infection that can sicken ducks. Infected ducks are often found on their backs, paddling their legs. Additionally, weight loss, intestinal disturbance and eye bubbling are also potential symptoms.

A vaccine exists for this condition, but antibacterial medications are often helpful for saving ducks with the disease.

Duck Viral Enteritis

Also referred to as "duck plague", this disease can cause ducks to die within a few hours of showing symptoms (Enzo R. Campagnolo, 2001). Your flock could be acting completely normal when you look in on them in the morning and be dead before you start eating lunch. Ducks appear to be particularly susceptible to this disease (S. Davison, 1993).

Symptoms of the infection include lethargy, anorexia, photophobia (aversion to bright lights), droopiness, nasal discharge and gastrointestinal upset. However, the most common first sign is a massive die off of ducks. This occurs periodically in wild waterfowl populations as well.

There is no treatment for viral enteritis. The only way to prevent the disease is to keep ducks from having contact with other ducks, practice strict hygiene and have all of your ducks vaccinated against the disease. However, the vaccine confers immunity very quickly, and can be used during an outbreak, if administered quickly enough.

Haemoproteus

Haemoproteus is a deadly respiratory infection that can infect Ducks. While Ducks are usually more disease-resistant than ducks, Ducks exhibit some innate immunity to the infection, while Ducks can catch the infection from symptomless Ducks (GALT, 1980).

Fowl Cholera

Fowl cholera is a bacterial infection that can infect Ducks. Caused by the bacteria Pasteurella multocida, the disease is highly contagious, and found in waterfowl populations worldwide.

Unfortunately, the symptoms of fowl cholera vary widely. In many cases, one of the first clues is the sudden die off of a large number of birds that were formerly without symptoms. When symptoms are present, they often include intestinal disturbance, rapid breathing, anorexia and depression.

Cholera is usually transmitted via water sources, such as wetlands and ponds. Fowl cholera is a zoonotic, so it is important to recognize the symptoms of the disease and seek treatment for the birds, as it can be transmitted to humans.

Antibiotics are usually prescribed to treat infected birds, but they do not always work. In a 1992 study, fowl cholera was fatal to approximately 50 percent of the birds in the study. The other half of the birds recovered after treatment with antibiotics (Nakamine M, 1992). However, many birds die after treatment stops, which shows that the disease has not been eliminated, but only suppressed.

When a flock is infected with Fowl Cholera, the area must be completely depopulated and cleaned thoroughly to prevent further infection.

Duck Parvovirus

Duck parvovirus is a disease that is especially dangerous to Ducks. In fact, the disease is sometimes called "Duck disease," or "Duck parvovirus." Primarily a disease of young Ducks, the virus does not cause symptoms in ducks older than five weeks of age.

When young ducks become infected with this deadly pathogen, they only have an approximately 20 percent chance of survival. Hatchlings and young ducklings transmit the virus between themselves, but ducks can also catch the virus from their mother.

Sick ducklings exhibit signs of nervousness, huddle together in a tight cluster and may drag their feet behind themselves. Digestive disturbances may also occur, although the birds do not lose feathers as geese do when infected with the goose parvovirus.

There is no treatment for the pathogen except establishing very strict quarantines and implementing a vaccination program. Day-old chicks can be vaccinated, but the adults must be given boosters regularly to prevent passing the virus to the young, and susceptible, ducklings.

3. Common Traumatic Injuries

Even if you keep your ducks' enclosure impeccably clean, have them vaccinated against common diseases and keep them separate from all other ducks, they can sustain traumatic injuries. Traumatic injuries are not always as dire as their name implies; they simply occur from an event, rather than a pathogen.

The best way to prevent traumatic injuries from occurring is through vigilantly inspecting their environment for potential hazards. By practicing good husbandry, you can reduce the chances of injury.

Frostbite

While Ducks often tolerate cold temperatures well, one of the first problems they are likely to experience in very cold temperatures is frostbite. Frostbite is easier to prevent than to treat, so always be sure that your ducks have a shelter that allows them to escape inclement weather. In extreme cases, frostbite can be fatal.

One of the reasons that Ducks are so susceptible to frostbite is that they are warm-climate ducks, who dip their heads frequently in the water. When they pull their heads back out, their delicate facial tissue is wet and exposed to the cold and wind. Their feet sustain damage when the ducks walk on cold, wet ground or snow for extended lengths of time.

If you see that your ducks feet, face or bill have areas that are black, cracked or ulcerated, visit your veterinarian for treatment and fortify their shelter to provide more warmth.

Abraded Feet

Although they look sturdy, the feet of Ducks are very sensitive to rough surfaces. In severe cases, the ducks can develop serious, systemic infections if the wounds are not cleaned and treated properly.

If you notice wounds or abrasions on your ducks' feet, take them to the veterinarian for treatment. Your veterinarian will likely clean the wound, apply some antibiotics and schedule a follow up exam.

After visiting your veterinarian, it is crucial to fix the problem to prevent further injury. Ensure that all surfaces that the ducks must walk on are smooth and clean to reduce the likelihood of complications.

It also may be necessary to keep your Duck in an enclosed space while he heals. The bacteria on the ground and in the water may cause the wounds to become infected.

Missing Feathers or Wounds

Ducks lose feathers for a variety of reasons, including infighting, poor nutrition and sickness. Additionally, ducks molt periodically to replace their feathers.

While the first molt you witness may cause you to be concerned, you will soon learn the cycle of molting and what it looks like when the birds go through the process.

However, it is important to distinguish normal molting (and incidental feather loss that happens from normal activity from time to time) from that associated with infighting or disease.

Visit your veterinarian if you cannot determine the cause of the lost feathers. Your veterinarian can perform tests to determine whether or not your duck is suffering from an illness. Missing feathers will usually re grow with the next molting cycle.

Tangled String and Similar Wounds

Ducks can become entangled in a number of man-made substances, including string, fishing line, rope, netting, plastic or wire. In some circumstances – such as when ducks become tangled while in the water – this can be a deadly problem. Because these types of problems often cause ducks to flail about and struggle frantically to escape, be alert for panicked, struggling ducks. However, if the duck is able to move about relatively normally, they may not exhibit high stress levels, and just try to make the best of the situation.

If you find that your duck is tangled, try to keep it calm while you work to remove the foreign material. Grasp the duck gently but firmly with your arm, while you work the string or wire off with the other hand. It often helps to have another person assist with the procedure.

If your duck is stressed or upset by the activity, it sometimes helps to cover his/her head with a soft, dark cotton bag or towel. Do not wrap it tightly around its head, but let it drape freely. Alternatively, you can take the duck to a dark area, which may also help to calm it down.

After removing all of the material, inspect the duck for wounds. Often, while attempting to free themselves, ducks cause fishing line or similar materials to cut into their skin. If any significant cuts are apparent, consider seeking veterinary attention as infection is a strong possibility.

If the wounds are minor, use a wound wash or clean water to cleanse the area. Keep the duck in a clean, dry, warm environment for a few days to ensure he/she heals without developing an infection.

Fixing a Broken Wing

The wings of Ducks form and important part of their defense mechanism and also help them maintain the balance of their bodies when they are running or walking upright. So, a broken wing is a serious issue that must be taken care of immediately.

Of course, you will require the assistance of a waterfowl vet to help take care of the issue completely. However, first aid is necessary when you have a duck with a broken wing to ensure that the condition does not become worse.

There are several reasons why a duck might have a broken wing. If the drakes become aggressive, they are capable of getting injured in fights. Mating among ducks is so aggressive that, many times, the female might be attacked by several males at one time and actually breaks her wings. In addition to this, an attack by a predator may also cause serious injuries to ducks. There are always chances of the wing getting stuck in wires or mesh, leading to injuries like broken bones. Whatever the cause, broken wings can be very painful and must be take care of at the earliest.

A broken wing can cause excruciating pain and can lead to a lot of stress if left unattended. Sometimes, broken wings may also be accompanied by serious cuts and wounds that need to be treated properly to avoid infections. So it is necessary for you to be able to identify a broken wing.

When a wing is broken, it will hang very low. You will notice that it is displaced and is much lower than the other wing.

The first step to treating a broken wing is to gain the confidence of the bird to be able to handle it. Usually when they are injured, birds tend to become more defensive. Especially after an attack, a duck will not really be very easy to hold and take into your care.

First, give the duck some feed and also some water. If he actually begins to eat, it is much easier for you to get a grip on it. However, after a traumatizing injury, your duck is less likely to want to eat. In such cases, the only option you have is to chase the duck to a corner and then catch it. You must be firm in your grip and must gently hold the wings down, taking great care with the broken wing. The best way to calm a duck down is to set her in an isolated spot or even a small cage which is well lit and warm.

You must approach an injured duck only when you are certain that it has calmed down completely. Failing this, you will find yourself going through the entire process of calming it down again.

Gently examine the bird for wounds and cuts that might be bleeding. These wounds must be washed to remove any impurity that might lead to infection. The wound can be washed with some lukewarm water or even iodine solution. If you have an antiseptic that you have used before, you may apply it.

138

The next step is to provide a splint or support of the broken wing. You can use sticky gauze or even veterinary tape for this purpose. Hold the wing in the natural position first. It must be held against the body of the bird to make sure that it heals in its natural position. Once the wing is in place, it needs to be bound to the body securely. Take the gauze or the tape around the body of the bird. The objective of the gauze and the tape is to ensure that the wing is immobilized. However, if you tie it too tightly, it might affect the breathing of the bird.

When you wrap the gauze, take it over the broken wing, around the body and under the wing that is functional. This will not restrict the movement of the other wing.

Usually, broken wings take about 4 weeks to heal completely. It is best that you keep the runner in a cage and in isolation until the wing is completely healed. The quality of food must be very good during the healing period. Plenty of water must also be available for the bird to drink. In this period, if the gauze or tape becomes soiled, you may change it.

While you are changing the gauze, if you notice that the duck is able to move the wing comfortably, you can remove the dressing. If not, you can take the gauze off after four weeks. Now your bird is also ready to mingle with the rest of the flock and carry on with his routine.

If your bird has been attacked by a predator, he might require vaccinations or shots to ensure that there is no infection. Even in case of open wounds, it is best recommended that you have it checked by a waterfowl professional.

4. Behavioral Problems

The most common behavior problems that occur in ducks are nipping, pinching and aggression. For most part, ducks are calm and complaisant creatures. Behavior problems usually occur only when the ducks are 6 months of age or older. Aggression is a common problem with drakes who are ready to mate.

It is necessary to curb this type of behavior in the initial years to ensure that it does not persist. If your duck shows any aggressive behavior, a stern and sharp, 'No' should do the trick. However, if the ducks are stubborn, you may also hold the bill and shake it gently, without causing damage to the neck or eyes while repeating a "No". Ducks take time to view their owners as trustworthy companions and not predators.

Stress is also a problem with Ducks. If you see your duck breathing with an open mouth, flapping his wings often and also refusing to interact with other ducks, there are chances that he is stressed. This may occur due to sudden change in location, extreme weather conditions or even health issues. Your vet will be able to diagnose this problem and provide necessary solutions.

5. Reproductive Diseases

Egg Binding

Egg binding can occur for a number of reasons. The formed egg may be too large to pass through the shell gland or the vagina, the duck may have hypocalcaemia (calcium deficiency) or it may have sustained injury to its vent or vagina.

This often occurs in birds that are of advanced age, extremely young age or are overweight. While the retained egg obstructs the passageway, the duck's body continues producing eggs behind it. Ultimately, this can lead to ruptures or eggs being deposited into the abdominal cavity.

Regardless of the reason it occurs, egg binding is a medical emergency. Ducks that are having difficulty expelling an egg may appear nervous, agitated or depressed. They may walk or pace excessively, as well as exhibit strange body postures.

Unfortunately, this condition is most often noted upon necropsy, as the birds often die before their owner has noticed the symptoms.

If you suspect that a female is egg bound, contact your veterinarian immediately.

Oviduct Prolapse

Sometimes, the oviduct protrudes in the lower region. This condition usually occurs when the duck has difficulty in passing the egg out.

Treatment:
- Provide calcium and phosphorous supplements
- Feed should only include layers pellets
- Keep the duck warm
- Oral medication or injections if the problem persists.

Exposed Penis

Usually, in Ducks the penis cannot be retracted causing it to drop externally from the body. This may head to infections if it persists. Waterfowl experts associate the upright position of the bird with this problem.

Treatment:
- Keep the environment sanitary and clean
- Provide the bird with lots of drinking water

Meritis

Bacterial infection of the oviduct, leading to inflammation is known as meritis.
Symptoms
- Persistent vaginal discharge
- Loss of appetite

- Lethargy

Treatment
- Antibodies administered orally or through injections

Peritonitis

Peritonitis is usually the result of an ovarian prolapse. When the egg fails to make its way into the oviduct but goes into the abdominal cavity instead, peritonitis occurs. The lining of the abdomen called the peritoneum gets infected.

Symptoms

- Swelling around the abdomen
- Diarrhea
- Sudden Death

Treatment
- Antibiotics have been effective in some cases.

Many breeders put their Ducks 'to sleep' when they show reproductive problems. Especially if the primary business is egg production, these ducks become a liability. Most breeders resort to this procedure as waterfowl vets can be quite expensive. However, if you are patient, you can help your duck get back to its normal self and produce healthy eggs.

6. Finding a Good Duck Veterinarian

Unfortunately, the veterinarian you take your dog or cat to may not be qualified to treat your Ducks. Fortunately, finding a veterinarian who specializes in farm animals or birds is not as hard to find as it was years ago.

To find a veterinarian, begin by asking the breeder, retailer or individual from whom you purchased the birds. Often, they will have a relationship with a veterinarian accustomed to caring for waterfowl. If that does not work, you can ask other duck hobbyists in your area.

If none of these strategies allows you to locate a vet, search the internet and local phone listings. If possible, search for reviews of the veterinarian before visiting him or her.

Remember that ducks are not dogs or cats, and a trip to the veterinarian can be an especially stressful event. Therefore, a veterinarian that makes house calls is especially helpful. However, your ducks may require hospitalization or surgery to remedy some illnesses, so it is important the veterinarian has access to a place suitable for such procedures.

Always locate and meet with your veterinarian soon after acquiring your flock. This way, you can become acquainted with the vet if you are not already, and your vet can give your ducks a preliminary physical to ensure they are healthy.

One of the other reasons to visit your veterinarian immediately after acquiring your ducks is to prevent the spread of any diseases they have to their new environment.

For example, if your newly purchased ducks have an illness, and you take them directly from the breeder to your pond, they may spread the disease throughout their enclosure.

Later, when you take them to the veterinarian and have them treated, you must then take them back to their enclosure, where they will become re-infected, thus necessitating further treatment. Additionally, you will be forced to clean the entire enclosure – including the water reservoir – from top to bottom.

Therefore, if at all possible, take the ducks directly from the place you acquire them to the veterinarian's office.

Many duck breeders will determine the gender of the ducks for you, if this is not possible, your veterinarian should be able to determine the gender of the birds for you.

Predatory Attack

While most predatory attacks are likely to end badly for your duck, some ducks do survive such encounters. These episodes have three different problems that must be overcome for the duck to survive.

Initially, the duck must survive the attack. Ducks may be killed from broken necks, damaged organs, profuse bleeding (which can occur internally) or simply from the shock of the attack. Once they have survived this, the duck will need your help to address any significant wounds.

Wash your duck with a veterinary-approved wound wash or, if none is available, clean water. If there are any major lacerations, obviously broken bones or similar symptoms, you must take your duck to the veterinarian immediately. Once these wounds are treated, the duck must survive the last threat from such encounters: infection.

During the healing process, it is important to keep the injured duck in a quiet, calm and clean habitat. Follow your veterinarian's instructions regarding access to swimming water, the administration of medications and any other follow up care.

While attacks are stressful events, with luck and prompt action, you may be able to help your duck survive the encounter.

Poisoning

While not a "traumatic event" by the strictest definition, poisoning should be handled in a similar manner. The symptoms of poisoning vary with the causative agent at work, and are often only determined after ruling out other possible problems.

One frequent cause of poisoning is moldy food. Many molds that grow on wet cereal grains can cause serious illness or death for birds that consume them. Alfatoxins are one of the most important types to prevent. Always ensure that your ducks food stays dry to prevent it from molding. Never feed ducks any food that may contain mold; if there is any doubt in the status of a given food, discard it and replace it with fresh food.

Botulism can occur if your ducks have access to stagnant, warm water, which allows the anaerobic bacteria Clostridium botulinum to thrive. Botulism usually produces a limp paralysis of the neck, wings and legs. Ducks usually lapse into a coma and die within two days of contracting the disease.

Additionally, several chemicals can be very toxic to ducks. Lead and zinc both cause muscle weakness, weight loss and digestive problems. Ducks may ingest lead in the form of old paint chips, lead shot or lead fishermen's weights. Zinc often comes from galvanized metal tubs and fixtures.

Mercury, which is derived from a variety of sources, (including the fish that the ducks eat) also causes weakness. Mercury may stay inside the duck's body (or inside the eggs they produce) for many months after ingestion.

Phosphorus, which is found in a number of rodent poisons, matches and fireworks can be especially deadly. While ducks sometimes exhibit weakness or depression upon ingesting phosphorus, they may also experience very sudden death, in which no symptoms occur.

Even relatively benign chemicals, such as salt, can cause health problems if ingested in large quantities. Salt used to de-ice roads often ends up at the bottom of the watershed – such as your duck's pond. If enough is ingested, ducks may experience convulsions, kidney failure or even death.

Arsenic is another potentially dangerous chemical that your ducks may come into contact with. Used in a variety of poisons, arsenic is also present in some treated lumber. However, if the lumber has dried completely, it will not leach into the environment and harm your ducks. Ducks that eat arsenic show signs of nervousness, and they often die.

Carbon monoxide is an odorless, colorless gas that is often created by heating units. Always be sure that your ducks' shelter is well ventilated if you use a heating device. Carbon monoxide can cause very rapid death in most animals, including ducks.

This chapter discusses some of the most common health issues that duck owners need to deal with. However, if you think that there are other symptoms that you duck might be exhibiting, make sure you take him to a water fowl expert at the earliest. Never neglect even the slightest abnormality in the health of your Duck.

The other thing to remember is that you must never provide home remedies and medicines for pets. In case of ducks and poultry you must be additionally cautious as they may have infections that affect our health, too. Make sure you take your duck for routine checkups to keep him in the pink of his health. In case you are negligent you will not only put your health at risk but will also have to shell out tones of money. Remember, taking care of the health of your duck is expensive as you require the services of specialized waterfowl vets. So the best thing to do is to keep your ducks healthy by providing them with a clean and healthy environment to live in.

Resources

Seek to continually learn more about your Ducks. As with the husbandry of all domestic animals, new techniques and strategies are developed constantly. Never turn down an opportunity to learn more about your new pets, and eagerly seek out those who may know more than you do about these big, beautiful birds.

1. Books

Books can provide information not found on internet chat rooms and message boards. Books are an especially valuable resource for finding biological information about the species.

Ducks, Geese and Swans: Species Accounts

Edited by Janet Kear

Oxford University Press, 2005

Diseases of Wild Waterfowl

By Gary A. Wobeser

Springer, 1997

Naturalized Birds of the World

By Christopher Lever

A&C Black 2010

Diseases of Poultry

Edited by David E. Swayne

John Wiley & Sons, 2013

Ducks and Geese: Standard Breeds and Management

By George Ellsworth Howard

U.S. Department of Agriculture, 1897

Biology of Breeding Poultry

By Paul M. Hocking

CABI, 2009

Ducks

By F. Bauer

Papua New Guinea, Department of Primary Industry, 1980

2. Websites

In the information age, learning more about your Ducks is only a few clicks away. Be sure to bookmark these sites for quick access in the future.

Informational Websites

Backyard Chickens

http://www.backyardchickens.com/

Though focused on chickens, this website and message board contains plenty of information about Ducks as well.

Poultry Hub

http://www.poultryhub.org/

Maintained by the Poultry Cooperative Research Centre, Poultry Hub provides information regarding all aspects of duck care.

Madiera Birdwatching

http://www.madeirabirds.com/

Madeira Birdwatching provides information about the birds commonly seen on the island, including Ducks.

South Florida ducks

http://www.southfloridaDuckducks.com/

This site includes information about wild, feral and captive Ducks.

Duck Central http://www.Duckduckcentral.com/

Information about the care and breeding of Ducks.

Backyard Poutry

http://www.backyardpoultrymag.com/

Online magazine featuring news, information and more concerning Ducks and other common poultry.

Ducks Unlimited

http://www.ducks.org/

The world's leading conservation organization dedicated to protecting ducks and their natural habitats.

Cornell Lab of Ornithology

http://www.birds.cornell.edu/

Information about most birds native to North America. This site provides identification photos, sample calls from most species and tips for spotting various species in the wild.

The Poultry Club of Great Britain

http://www.poultryclub.org/

This website provides a variety of helpful resources, as well as information about poultry husbandry and breeding. You can also use this website to find information on breed standards, competitions and meet other poultry enthusiasts.

Xeno-Canto

http://www.xeno-canto.org/

Based in the Netherlands, xeno-canto is a repository for birds sounds, collected from around the world.

Beauty of Birds

http://beautyofbirds.com/

Beauty of Birds has information on Ducks, including information about feral colonies.

The Bird Hotline

http://www.birdhotline.com/

A wealth of information is available on this site. While most is oriented towards parakeets and similar birds, the veterinary resources provided on the website are of value to Duck keepers.

Breeders

Duck breeders are not only an excellent source for purchasing hatchlings; they can also provide a wealth of information. Please note that I have bought any ducks from all of these breeders. Make sure that you investigate them thoroughly before buying ducks from them.

Al's Quackery

http://alsquackery.weebly.com/

Al's Quakery has plentiful information regarding Duck care and color mutations. Additionally, the Quakery offers Ducks for sale when they are available.

J. M. Hatchery

http://www.jmhatchery.com/

J. M. Hatchery breeds and sells a variety of poultry species, including white Ducks.

CaliforniaHatchery.com

http://www.californiahatchery.com/

CaliforniaHatchery.com sells a wide variety of ducks, chickens and other poultry.

Cheap Chicks Poultry Farm

http://cheapchickpoultryfarm.weebly.com/

Cheap Chicks Poultry Farm sells hatchlings and eggs of Ducks and many other poultry breeds.

Metzer Farms

http://www.metzerfarms.com/

Metzer Farms hatches a variety of bird species, and their website provides information about Duck housing, maintenance and feeding.

University and Governmental Resources

University of Texas at El Paso

https://www.utep.edu/

The University of Texas, El Paso website contains a great deal of duck-oriented information. Of special note are the bird taxonomy resources, which provide information about the classification of ducks.

University of California, Davis

http://animalscience.ucdavis.edu/

UC Davis works extensively with livestock (including poultry), and they work to enhance the lives of captive and companion animals through science.

Duck Research Laboratory

http://www.duckhealth.com/

Maintained by the Cornell University College of Veterinary Medicine, this site provides a wealth of information regarding the husbandry of ducks, including Ducks.

The Poultry Site

http://www.thepoultrysite.com/

Although primarily focused on turkeys and chickens, this Oklahoma State University maintained website contains some information about Ducks.

Animal Diversity Web

http://animaldiversity.ummz.umich.edu/

Maintained by the University of Michigan, the Animal Diversity Web has thousands of pages of information, detailing the lives of various animal species. In addition to reading about Ducks, you can also learn about their predators, prey and competitors here.

Center for Integrated Agricultural Systems

http://www.cias.wisc.edu/

This page, provided and maintained by the University of Wisconsin-Madison, contains a wealth of data concerning all common farm animals, including Ducks.

The Centers for Disease Control and Prevention

http://www.cdc.gov/

Based in Atlanta, Georgia, the CDC provides information on a variety of diseases that may be zoonotic. Additionally, the website provides further resources for coping with outbreaks of salmonella.

Veterinary Resources

Veterinarians.com

http://www.localvets.com/

This site is a search engine that can help you find a local veterinarian to treat your Ducks.

European Committee of the Association of Avian Veterinarians

http://www.eaavonline.org/

This website includes a veterinarian locator, as well as a long list of links that may be useful for Duck owners.

All About Birds

www.allaboutbirds.org/guide/Duck/id

A comprehensive website that covers various subjects like life history, care and breeding of different domestic birds.

NC Wildlife

www.ncwildlife.org

A special compilation of Duck facts and figures.

AvianBiotech.com

http://www.avianbiotech.com/Index.htm

AvianBiotech.com provides DNA-based lab services to bird owners.

Association of Avian Veterinarians

http://www.aav.org/

In addition to being a good resource for finding a qualified avian veterinarian, this site provides information on veterinary colleges, bird health and basic care.

For The Birds

http://www.forthebirdsdvm.com/

Veterinary and care information for all birds, as well as specific care advice for ducks.

References

- Centers for Disease Control and Prevention . (2014). *http://www.cdc.gov/features/salmonellapoultry/*. Retrieved from   CDC.gov: http://www.cdc.gov/features/salmonellapoultry/

- Enzo R. Campagnolo, M. B. (2001). An Outbreak of Duck Viral Enteritis (Duck Plague) in Domestic Ducks (Cairina moschata domesticus) in Illinois. *Avian Diseases.*

- Fernando GogliAntonia Lanni, C. D.-L. (1993). Effect of cold acclimation on oxidative capacity and respiratory properties of liver and muscle mitochondria in ducklings, Cairina moschata. *Comparative Biochemistry and Physiology Part B: Comparative Biochemistry.*

- GALT, R. J. (1980). MORTALITY IN DUCKS (Cairina moschata) CAUSED BY Haemoproteus INFECTION. *Journal of Wildlife Diseases.*

- Hilary S. Stern, D. (2014). *Care and Feeding of Pet Ducks*. Retrieved from For The Birds: http://www.forthebirdsdvm.com/pages/care-and-feeding-of-pet-ducks

- KATARZYNA KLECZEK, E. W.-W. (2007). Effect of body weights of day-old Ducklings on growths . *Arch. Tierz., Dummerstorf.*

- Kear, J. (2005). *Ducks, Geese and Swans: Species accounts (Cairina to Mergus)*. Oxford University Press.

- Lack, D. (n.d.). The proportion of yolk in the eggs of waterfowl. *Wildfowl.*

- Larry R. McDougald, P. (2012). *Overview of Coccidiosis in Poultry*. Retrieved from The Merck Veterinary Manual: http://www.merckmanuals.com/vet/poultry/coccidiosis/overview_of_coccidiosis_in_poultry.html

- Mail, D. (2012). That's quite a bill! Prize-winning Duck drake becomes Britain's most expensive duck after fetching £1,500 at auction . *Daily Mail.*

- *Major Viral Diseases of Waterfowl and Their Control.* (2011). Retrieved from The Poultry Site: http://www.thepoultrysite.com/articles/2051/major-viral-diseases-of-waterfowl-and-their-control

- Mutinelli, I. C. (2001). Mortality in Ducks (Cairina moschata) and domestic geese (Anser anser var. domestica) associated with natural infection with a highly pathogenic avian influenza virus of H7N1 subtype. *Avian Pathology* .

- Nakamine M, O. M. (1992). The first outbreak of fowl cholera in Ducks (Cairina moschata) in Japan. *The Journal of Veterinary Medical Science / the Japanese Society of Veterinary Science.*

- S. Davison, K. A. (1993). Duck Viral Enteritis in Domestic Ducks in Pennsylvania. *Avian Diseases.*

- SORENSO, K. P. (1999). PHYLOGENY AND BIOGEOGRAPHY OF DABBLING DUCKS (GENUS: ANAS): A COMPARISON OF MOLECULAR AND MORPHOLOGICAL EVIDENCE . *The Auk* .

- Stai, S. M. (2004). Promiscuity and sperm competition in Ducks, Cairina moschata. *University of Miami Library.*

- That's quite a bill! Prize-winning Duck drake becomes Britain's most expensive duck after fetching £1,500 at auction . (2012). *Daily Mail.*

- Tzschentke, B., & Nichelmann, M. (2000). Influence of age and wind speed on total effective ambient temperature in three poultry species

Published by IMB Publishing 2014

158

CPSIA information can be obtained
at www.ICGtesting.com
Printed in the USA
BVHW071814120321
602296BV00007B/673